AMERICAN AFFAIR

 **Susan Marling** is a writer and broadcaster who specialises in travel and social documentary. She lives in London but goes to America for sharp talk, power showers and the guiltless pleasure of valet parking.

 **Gerd Kittel** is one of the world's top photographers. His books include studies of the American landscape and its road culture. He is involved in several events concerning contemporary photography, among them the European Photography Award by Deutsche Leasing AG.

AMERICAN AFFAIR

THE AMERICANISATION OF BRITAIN

SUSAN MARLING   PHOTOGRAPHS BY GERD KITTEL

BOXTREE

in association with

Carlton Television · The Principal Film Company · Vamp Films

The television series *American Affair* is
produced by The Principal Film Company with Vamp Films
for Carlton Television
First published in Great Britain in 1993 by Boxtree Limited

Designed by Martin Lovelock

Printed and bound in Great Britain by Bath Press for
Boxtree Limited
Broadwall House
21 Broadwall
London SE1 9PL

A CIP catalogue entry for this book is available from the British Library.

ISBN 1 85283 460 9

Contents

What's so special about this relationship?

Don't get me wrong. Some of my best friends and relations are Americans. I think America sometimes gets a rough ride in Britain, characterised as home of the serial killer, the therapy junkie, the cabbage-patch doll collector, the fornicating evangelist, the Miami matron, the brain-dead redneck, the weirdo – 'Houston Man Marries His Dog'. We are too often content to portray America as bizarre and out of control – it makes us feel smug and stable and able to mutter about the things that 'could never happen here'. Nevertheless, communications and travel have brought the two countries closer than ever in the shrinking global village. America may not be sending us the undiluted madness that so pleases the tabloids – but there's a brisk transatlantic trade in almost everything else. In business, architecture and retailing, in the food, clothing and service industries and in entertainment and culture, America is a detectable force in this country. So we may as well have a go at understanding our ambivalence about that.

> *For other nations, Utopia is a blessed past, never to be recovered; for Americans it is just beyond the horizon.*
>
> HENRY KISSINGER

The power of American influence in Britain was brought home to me at a London bus stop by a bloke in a jeans jacket. He was young, a snappy dresser, with a well-tended quiff and sideburns shaved to surgical points. As he stepped in front of me to get on the bus, I saw that on the back of his jacket there was embossed a single word: AMERICA.

Somehow those seven letters were enough to give added value to the jacket and to suggest to passers-by that the wearer was not your ordinary jeans-jacket man but – what? Wilder, more glamorous, adventurous; more of a Harley Davidson-riding, James Dean sort of a guy. To have BRITAIN or ENGLAND written on your back (unless you are a thug looking for

American graffiti: our love affair with '50s America is influenced more by popular film and TV images like *Grease* or *Happy Days* than by the reality.

Swedish football supporters) would be unthinkable. But the word AMERICA gives proxy membership of that fabulous, brawling, hyper-energetic great mayhem of a nation. Not a bad feeling to have on the top of a double-decker bus headed for Shepherd's Bush.

Some of our excitement (or fear) about America is to do with how we feel about the future. It often seems that innovation – the latest technology, research, fad, fashion or miracle cure – comes to us directly from America. We look across a five-hour time zone and hope to see something of how we'll be (if we're lucky, or if we're not careful, depending on your point of view) in five years' time. Of course, we're not always right in crediting the United States with stealing a march on the future. The biggest movers and shakers in communications and industry are supranational now, and there are those who look at China and the energy of the new Far Eastern and Latin American economies and wonder if the American Empire is waning …

> *Americans are better at having a love affair that lasts ten minutes than anyone else on earth.*
>
> STEPHEN SPENDER

But America has a few good jeans jacket-selling years left. The imagery associated with the United States is still potent. According to Charles Garland of the advertising agency Bartle, Bogle, Hegarty (who make the Levi's adverts and were therefore indirectly responsible for selling the jeans jacket to your man on the double-decker), the appeal of America has persisted because, selectively, we choose to believe in the American Dream. Anyone unfamiliar with the Dream will find help in the *Encyclopaedia Britannica*:

> A democratic land of opportunity, in which social, political, economic
> and religious freedom prevail, one person is as good as another
> and individuals can achieve their dream if only they work hard enough.

The compacted roots of this Dream can be epitomised in relatively few images. BBH has assembled a series of film clips that highlight these saleable, positive aspects of America, the backdrop that advertisers have used so successfully. It begins with a few frames of the pioneer life – the move west and the forging of a nation, against an awesome, magnificent landscape. There are some wholesome family scenes, fishing and baseball, apple pie and snow at Christmas. A couple more scenes catalogue the prodigiously quick growth of US economic, and space (but not military) power and then we're into the 1950s and 1960s and that skyscraping urban landscape that matches the natural one for sheer chutzpah. The survival of a brave, hardworking individual is implied in every scene.

We encounter these images of American expansiveness and freedom not just through advertising, but via film, television and music. As BBH puts it: 'America is the source of the dream. And American-controlled media are the filter.' No greater proof of this is needed than the *Screen International* list of the top ten films we watched in the United Kingdom in 1992:

1 Basic Instinct (US)
2 Hook (US)
3 Lethal Weapon 3 (US)
4 Batman Returns (US)
5 The Addams Family (US)
6 Cape Fear (US)
7 Beauty and the Beast (US)
8 Wayne's World (US)
9 My Girl (US)
10 The Hand That Rocks the Cradle (US)

What we in Britain are encouraged to do is to 'access' bits of the American Dream and its associated values (service, honesty, directness, wholesomeness and optimism) through consumption. Certain brands of clothing (Levi's), footwear (Nike), alcohol (Southern Comfort/Budweiser), cigarettes (Marlboro) as well as some foods, services and 'lifestyle products', exploit the Dream to full advantage.

The trouble is that the Dream is highly selective. It can't, for example, be made to work on contemporary US cars – Europeans would rather buy German. It won't work on *haute couture* or *cuisine*, interior design, furniture and so on. What's more, BBH and others acknowledge that advertisers must steer clear of the negative images of America which threaten to pop up and turn the Dream into a nightmare. 'Best to avoid anything that might portray America as the global policeman,' Charles Garland advises. Indeed, any developments post *Easy Rider* seem difficult to accommodate in Dream-based advertising. So we are left with ambivalence: half in love with the Dream but conscious of its limitations.

US influence leaves us everywhere in two minds. In speech we admire the Americans for their independence of attitude, their self-assertion and urban smart talk. We like them for being vigorous, freewheeling and frank. We accept their criticism of our diffidence and have been trying harder to answer

The American fashion dream is taking over … everyone wears jeans, sweatshirts, T-shirts etc. We are witnessing a triumph of basics.

THE INDEPENDENT, 1992

11

(Above) These days we recognise the fast food chain before we recognise what street we are in.

(Right) Indian Nights: advertisers remind us that we can taste the American Dream. Well, in a cigarette at least.

back in shops and to adopt a bit of their approachable but firm 'call-me-Bob' management style.

On the other hand, we resist the American tendency to blurt out intimacies too quickly. We sometimes find the tendency of middle-class Americans to talk about their emotional problems (and analysis) rather squirm-making, especially when the psycho-babble hits you before you've ordered the first bottle of mineral water.

In Britain, despite this resistance, we have absorbed some of this kind of speech almost without being aware of it. Here are the words from a greetings card produced by the Blue Mountain company of Boulder, Colorado, and on sale in British card shops. Inside this 'Forgive Me' card it says:

> Forgive me for my faults that seem to follow my life. Forgive me for my insecurities that have caused you hurt and pain. It can be hard to bear. I love you and I'm sorry but remember that my heart needs your smiles and laughter …

And so on.

13mg TAR 0·9mg NICOTINE
SMOKING CAUSES CANCER
Health Departments' Chief Medical Officers

There's the same ambivalence about American food. We've learned something from the joyfully eclectic mixture of ethnic styles in the United States (where else would you encounter 'the Italian restaurant with the Spanish name hosted by the Jewish couple and their Greek partner featuring American steaks, French onion soup, Ecuadorian ceviche and Swiss fondue'?). On the other hand, plenty of American food is either heavy with foodie pretension or simple to the point of being a finger snack.

We may admire the attitude Americans take towards ageing and the fact that they clearly think death is optional. We are beginning to follow them in their example of working to delay the signs of age, in their preoccupation with health, aerobics, bran, plastic surgery and regular cruise holidays. We see the moral and economic sense behind taking 'grey power' seriously. Yet we balk when we see Nancy and Ronnie holding hands.

> *In America you watch TV and think that's totally unreal, then you step outside and it's just the same.*
>
> JOAN ARMATRADING

Even the legendary Special (political) Relationship between the two countries has been marked by this ambivalence. At the height of the back-slapping, complimentary-speech-making days of the Reagan/Thatcher administrations, a subversive poster appeared in Britain. It was an old *Gone With the Wind* movie poster but the heads of Clark Gable and Vivien Leigh had been cut out and replaced by the heads of state. Mutually ravished, Ronnie and Maggie were locked in an embrace against the war-torn landscape, a perfect image of the Special Relationship.

In fact the affair between Britain and the United States (like that between Rhett and Scarlett), has been a bit of a bumpy old business and, since 1945, not at all a partnership between equals. Churchill, in a sentimental, bond-restoring speech in 1954, was able to refer to:

> The majesty of the unwritten alliance which binds the British Commonwealth and Empire to the great Republic of the United States. We have history, law, philosophy; we have sentiment and common interest; we have language. We are often in agreement on current events and we stand on the same foundation of the supreme realities of the modern world.

But recently the relationship has been based on a fundamental fallacy: that Britain has enough power to affect American international decisions. She does not. Hence, while Britain may have been a comfortable ally during the Cold War and the United States may have shared its nuclear secrets with Britain during those years, we're on the sidelines when it comes to super-power decision-making. The Special Relationship tied Britain to American policies, sometimes against her interests and political instincts; it prolonged an illusion of power which had vanished; and it aided American economic expansion at her expense. Mrs T. allowed US planes to take off from Britain to bomb Gaddafi's Libya – yet at the same time she was worried that the US, ignoring the Atlantic Alliance, might shaft Britain by doing a deal with the USSR regardless of the European allies. President Clinton's foreign policy towards Bosnia and Iraq does not meet with universal cries of support in this country, where it often seems that America's slogan for foreign intervention is: 'If a thing's worth doing, it's worth overdoing.'

Americans think of themselves collectively as a huge rescue squad on twenty-four-hour call to any spot on the globe where dispute or conflict may erupt.

ELDRIDGE CLEAVER, 1968

For most of us, American influence has much more to do with the efforts which are currently being made to stage baseball matches at Lords than with a special political understanding between the countries. However, to understand how the United States has come to be a major player in our cultural life in Britain we have to turn the clock back … to that Dream Decade, the 1950s.

tops, the red and white steering wheels and the fins were magic. In America they had cars that were pale blue and bright pink, cars in which young people had fun, jumping in sometimes without opening the doors and then driving off with the wind in their hair. It was bewitching and, in Britain, still a vivid folk memory (even for those born after the 1950s).

If the plentiful consumer culture of the early 1950s sent Britain into a wave of imitative activity (you could, eventually, buy a Ford Popular in pale blue with white-walled tyres), it was nothing compared to the massive surge in youth culture that hit the country like a transatlantic tidal wave in the mid-1950s.

The year 1956 must be the one in which our American affair was consummated. It was certainly the first year of the transatlantic telephone service. Once again Britain was in the doldrums, having made a humiliating mess of the Suez Crisis (no support from America, despite the affair), and was watching gloomily as Poland and Hungary tried unsuccessfully to free themselves from Soviet influence.

Teenagers had been invented (just) but popular entertainment and distraction were still pretty safe – as the *Daily Telegraph* confirmed:

> Film of the year is *High Society*, which combines the cool elegance of
> Grace Kelly with the eye-rolling charm of Louis Armstrong and features
> an amusing duet for Bing Crosby and Frank Sinatra 'Did You Evah?'
> Miss Kelly's chief competitor in the coolness stakes is Deborah Kerr
> as the English governess in *The King and I*.

And then along came Bill. In 1956 Bill Haley and the Comets came to England and played to rapturous audiences at the Dominion Theatre (where at the time of writing *Grease* is playing – *plus ça change*). A newspaper reported that record sales had reached twenty-two million and that during Bill's act

> as an added attraction the saxophonist kneels on stage to play his
> instrument, while the bass player rides astride his bass. One Haley
> song title has become a catch-phrase 'See You Later, Alligator' to
> which the reply is 'In a While, Crocodile'. These greetings are
> said to be popular in Princess Margaret's set.

When the rapidly made film called *Rock Around the Clock* was shown later in the year gangs of Teddy boys, wearing bootlace ties and long, velvet-trimmed jackets like so many card sharps from American Westerns, ripped

The neon culture stressed the American ability to make selling attractive and, above all, obvious.

the seats from a cinema at the Elephant and Castle and went on the rampage. Some provincial towns responded by banning the film. Now it was official … Teenagers were Trouble and rock 'n' roll (which nobody ever mentioned was the black American expression for sexual intercourse) was Dangerous.

Fat little Bill Haley, of course, with his tartan tuxedo and his damp kiss-curl, was only the early warning. Back in the USA they were getting ready to test and be knocked out by a nuclear explosion called Elvis Presley, the white boy 'who could sing coloured'. In 1956 Presley was at the very beginning of his career. His first internationally released record, 'Heartbreak Hotel' ('Ah'm-ah sah lonelah baybah'), came out in January and, to everyone's astonishment, topped every record chart around the world.

Together with Marlon Brando and James Dean (who epitomised mixed-up youth – misunderstood, rebellious, yet loyal in friendship), Presley formed a triumvirate of new American heroes. Young people in Britain had their (British) jukeboxes and (Italian) Gaggia coffee machines but the influence, the stars and most of the hot records were from the States. Would that there could have been drive-in restaurants, soda fountains, diners and

North London's '50s music revival. The Metrotones are recognised as Europe's number one doo-wop outfit.

drugstores too. We had to wait for Disney and clever themed-restaurant owners to recreate the 1950s' teen culture we never had.

If you were young and working class in the 1950s there was nothing to beat the United States and its rock 'n' roll music. George Melly explained the spark that set a whole generation aflame:

> I think it had to do with military service. There was no point in getting on with your life after leaving school and while waiting to be called up. So they earned high wages in dead-end jobs and wanted something to spend them on. In this gap rock 'n' roll flourished.

But American influence wasn't limited to working-class youngsters. Coming out of 1950s America was the music of jazz artists like Miles Davis, Charlie Parker and Thelonious Monk whose records were essential listening for students in duffel-coat days. Kerouac, Ginsberg and Burroughs were the voices of the Beat Generation whose new hip language, fondness for the open road, drugs and easy sex were the forerunners of the 1960s' hippy revolution. Their dislike for whatever was 'square' behaviour, their deep restlessness, indifference to the past and a readiness to turn to Eastern philosophy (especially Zen) was reflected in Britain not only in our one 'beat' writer, Colin Wilson, whose book *The*

All over the world people were in love with the life of the American teenager. It was so much freer than it was anywhere else. On Saturday nights the drive-in was the automobile meeting ground where carloads of boys and girls would go to do anything from picking up each other to picking a fight.

TOM WOLFE

Outsider enjoyed considerable success, but, more important, in a generation of rock musicians whose lyrics and lifestyle were a tribute to the Beat Movement.

In the 1950s America seemed to be the driving engine behind events. (US foreign policy was, by the Cold War period, one of open intervention to protect the American way.) It was driving ideas and driving popular culture in a way it hasn't done since.

In later years other countries captured our imagination. The early 1960s were marked by a flirtation with the Italian *dolce vita* – with Vespas and dapper jackets. The French put on a film show which reminded us that they could be witty and incisive and politically outspoken, while in the latter part of the decade we were happy to be deafened by our own globally popular music and the news of our cultural renaissance.

But in the 1950s America had it, and was out in front by a mile. It's no wonder then that in our national album so many of the shots of America are from those first heady days of the affair. That is the period we choose to remember now. American retro – diner and drugstore, jukebox and bobbysox – may strike post-modern Americans as having as little to do now with *their* culture as Beefeaters have to do with *ours*, but love (especially among the elderly) is blind.

Scenes from a mall

When, in the year 2393, some young archaeologist is laser-scanning the rubble of our civilisation, let's hope he finds the remains of the Lakeside shopping mall in Thurrock, Essex. It will be a pretty exciting discovery – an authentic, late twentieth-century, American-style retail complex that says a lot about who we were, just as the city walls, the palaces, cathedrals, town halls and railway stations of the past thousand years have spoken volumes about our history until now.

He'll know from documentary evidence that in the 1990s Lakeside and similar malls replaced parks as the most popular weekend venues for families, that they accounted for 20 per cent of Britain's retail trade (some £20 billion) and that, following the American lead, they drew shoppers with restaurants, crèches, ice-rinks, tenpin-bowling halls, cinema complexes, indoor theme parks, gymnasiums and a small army of people doing mime. He might wonder why people in the 1990s needed to do their shopping in a place where there was a *monorail* (Merry Hill, Dudley, West Midlands) and a sort of constant, airport whooshy noise from the endless play of fountains and music, but what the hell? He should have found out that in our age, thanks largely to the USA, shopping stopped being a trudge down the high street on narrow pavements past Dorothy Perkins and Timothy Whites, and became instead an easy riding, easy parking, clean, all weather, Leisure Experience.

You can't have everything you want. Where would you put it all?

AMERICAN T-SHIRT SLOGAN

We have bought the American way of shopping and with it the creed: shopping is power. Shopping is the act that most clearly defines our capitalist society. When the Soviet empire began to crumble you can bet that it wasn't the prospect of democracy or disarmament that hastened the process – it was a craving for the mall, our groaning halls of goodies. Why,

Scenes from Thurrock Mall.

here were people who had seen magazines perhaps but could only guess at what Knickerbox and Next, Woolworth and Laura Ashley kept in store for Westerners under the cantilevered glass roofs of their shopping centres. When Boris Yeltsin entered an American supermarket for the first time it was widely reported that he had tears in his eyes as he looked along the 160 foot (50 metre) aisles, each devoted to a single type of food.

And a desire to join in the big shopping bonanza isn't confined to would-be consumers beyond the old iron curtain. The MetroCentre in Gateshead (360 shops, 12,000 free parking places, fifty restaurants, twenty-five million shoppers every year) attracts Norwegians, Swedes, people from *Iceland*, for heaven's sake, who travel over with empty suitcases and make a weekend holiday out of shopping for toothpaste and soap and shampoo (which, apparently, are very expensive in Scandinavia). When this curious trawl for toiletries is over, in the Garden Court (with 'luscious greenery and waterfalls'), the Roman Forum ('an elegant themed area offering stylish boutiques and unusual gifts with Classical-styled Tavernetta') and the Antique Village ('A typical English village offering quaint specialist shops clustered round the village pond and olde worlde teashop with water wheel'), the people from Scandinavia are free to amuse themselves.

Because the MetroCentre is more than just a shopping centre. John Hall, who conceived it, took his cue from the great malls of North America, where 'shopping is a pleasure and a major leisure activity'. Inspired by the now legendary West Edmonton Mall (831 shops with theme park, 125 eating opportunities, a dolphinarium and the largest indoor golf course in the world), Hall called in a North American design consultancy and asked it to build a 'retail revolution' in which the fun is fundamental. So, for seven days a week (though it is owned by the Church Commissioners), the MetroCentre is open for retail-with-leisure. Twenty-eight lanes of bowling, ten cinema screens and, in what's known as the Kingdom of King Whiz, a self-contained fairground 'including the Galaxy Express Roller Coaster, flying galleon, dodgem cars and exhilarating whirly chairs. Plus younger children's enjoyment in the Wizard's castle, the steam carousel and sailing the model boats.'

So where did it come from, the hyper-real shopping mall? Ironically, in common with much of what seems most American in our society, we had it first in Europe and exported it, only to watch the idea come boomeranging back across the Atlantic with a following wind of New World energy and a promise of success.

The mall has its roots in the early nineteenth-century arcades which were built to house luxury shops and cafés for the bourgeoisie who arrived in their carriages and hansom cabs. Cast-iron engineering allowed the galleries to be lofty and the glazed roofs let in the daylight and kept the rain off the promenading shoppers down below. Burlington Arcade and the Royal Opera Arcade off Pall Mall are surviving examples of the type. Distant cousins of the modern shopping mall, they now represent the very opposite retail culture – one where exclusivity, tradition and mahogany-panelled Englishness are the hallmarks.

The Yankee version of the mall came into being in modern America's dawning decade, the 1950s. Land was cheap, car ownership (with fins if possible) was on a rapid incline, there was full employment and money to spend. Victor Gruen, the architect widely credited as 'the father of the mall', hoped that the shopping centres he designed would eventually become proper social centres in the rapidly growing suburbs – a series of focal points in the hundreds of square miles of 'ticky tacky boxes', sprinkled lawns and criss-cross highways. The dream didn't come true. The malls remained unashamedly commercial and, ugly though many of the early models were, the British just couldn't wait for post-war austerity to be over so that we could start replicating them here. Sadly, by the time that happened it was the 1960s and concrete and brutalism were all the rage. In developing the (partly bomb-damaged) city centres a nasty rash of Arndale Centres began to appear. Without even the unlimited parking and spaciousness of the American counterparts, our new shopping centres quickly revealed themselves as windy, soulless places which were about as interesting as a paper cup in terms of their design. In comparison with the new, born-again British malls of the late 1980s and 1990s, they were dirty, dingy, depressing and much in need of what many of them now face – demolition.

And then there was Lakeside and the new wave of American retail wisdom. Suddenly we're in *Scenes from a Mall* starring Woody Allen and Bette Midler. In this little post-modern comedy of manners a couple plan to celebrate their seventeenth wedding anniversary with a dinner party

Shopping malls, Disneyland, television, are all examples of the new stage of hyper-reality – the falseness that is better than reality. Reality always has its detrimental aspects like crime, homeless people, dirt. In a situation of hyper-reality like a shopping mall, everything is reduced to a set of agreed upon themes, so people feel more comfortable here than in a real situation. The accurate urban reality is replaced by the falsehood of the shopping mall.

MARGARET CRAWFORD,
ARCHITECTURAL HISTORIAN

and so find themselves queuing for the mall car park (plenty of mobile telephone time) and for the takeaway sushi bar in Bullocks, a glorious cathedral of the American way of life. During an eventful shopping session they make their confessions, split up, buy a surfboard, get serenaded by a sombrero band, eat frozen yoghurt, dance in a champagne and piano bar, visit a stress management centre, buy clothes from a Turkish bazaar, watch an Indian film (and have sex on the cinema floor during the best scene), reaffirm their marriage and give a bloody nose to … a mime artist. The mall is their private place and a spectacular arena for their domestic violence.

Scenes from a Mall catches perfectly the pace and the luxurious fantasy of mall life. In the mall there's nothing odd about wandering into a restaurant done out as the Starship Enterprise, coming out and finding a choir of men in stovepipe hats singing carols about figgy pudding and then stepping into a fashion shop modelled on a fur trappers' trading post. The unending juxtaposition of spectacle and style gives you a sore head after a while, even if you're not having a relationship crisis with your shopping partner. It's just that shopping malls, carnivals of consumption, are a bit like theme parks, with the shopper in the role of gob-smacked tourist. This is what The Southern Belle, Lakeside's 'spectacular floating restaurant in the form of a replica Mississippi Paddle Steamer', is all about. It may be absurd in its setting and be a pastiche which bears little relationship to the original but it's fun and people seem to enjoy their 'Cajun chicken with tagliatelle', 'Swiss cheese and mushroom burger' and 'Moules marinière with Texas garlic toast' in these surroundings.

Of course, *Scenes from a Mall* is hyper-hyper-reality and no one could expect to spend such an exciting, action-packed day at Lakeside. Nevertheless people's behaviour at Lakeside is far from being entirely rational. Lakeside and its mall clones round the country are not places where you go to stride purposefully about and make sensible purchases from a list in your pocket. No, American retail is cleverer than that and they've passed a few tricks on to us. Whether we know it or not, retailers are interested not only in achieving 'high footfall figures' (translated as getting customers through the door for any reason) but also in increasing our 'dwell time' (hanging about, drifting, loitering).

(Previous page) The American influence can be seen on any supermarket shelf, from cereals and Coke to Bar-B-Q supplies and TV munchies for couch potatoes.

Young people are good at spending 'dwell time' in malls, lounging about in tribes that the Americans call 'mall-rats' and 'mall-bunnies'. In the United States sociologists claim that teenagers now *come of age* in the mall. Free from the scrutiny of parents or teachers it's where they first go in a car, where they first use a charge card, where they hang out, respond to fashion (and decide on the T-shirt, shoes or cap that identifies them as a preppy or a greeny or a rapper or a post-punk). It's where they check out the opposite sex and, according to several surveys, the parking lot of the mall is a favourite place for them to lose their virginity. In short, the mall is where they decide who they wanna be.

The attraction of the mall here and in America is partly about voyeurism. We're 'just looking' in the shops and at each other. You don't have to spend money and, because so many shops open straight on to the walking areas, you don't formally have to cross a threshold in a way that commits you to buying something. Malls seem to be very democratic places, open to all to watch, window shop and while away the time. And we're free, apparently, to choose what we do. (For Americans choice is the same as freedom – it might almost be written into the Constitution. Britain, remember, is a country where until very recently ice-cream only came in three flavours, and passion fruit wasn't one of them.)

If you think the US has stood still, who built the largest shopping centre in the world?

RICHARD NIXON

So how much choice do we really have? We don't have a complete choice of goods to buy in the mall because most of the shops there only sell goods in certain sectors – fashions, gifts, cards, sports goods, confectionery (not much of which is basic or necessary). We're given the choice between extremely specialised shops – drop in at Nail Perfection at Lakeside for the full range of polish and extensions, or perhaps Jigsaw World – and the same old chain-store names that you find in every shopping complex in the country. (In Britain the multiples or chain stores control 55 per cent of the total market in clothing, footwear and household goods.) Compare this US and UK uniformity with what happens in France and Italy, where each town has its unique collection of shops run by shopkeepers who live in the town, know their customers and know what they want.

Increasingly, as dedicated mall-bunnies will tell you, choice is limited because what shops sell is THE SAME.

It may look as though Lakeside's eight sports equipment shops are offering a huge range of goods but the same trainers turn up in each, more or less. All *we're* left with is making tiny distinctions between the sole, lace, tongue or air cushion of one trainer or the next. Or we can buy on the basis of (a) what TV adverts have announced as *the* desirable brand, or (b) a high price

Just like fast food chains, supermarket groups have cloned themselves throughout the country.

alone as a way of adding value to the shoes. Take this story: when trainers first began to sell in real bulk, Shop Number One was making a killing selling the hottest range, Nike Air Jordans, for £65. Their rival, Shop Number Two, unable to get its hands on further stock, bought them retail in the United States and priced them £30 higher. The result? Shop Number One's sales slumped. All the kids wanted to know what was wrong with Number One's shoes because they cost so little.

Do we have choice about how we behave? We're allowed our dwell time in the mall but we're also kept on the move by subtle means. Lakeside is built, like many malls, on the North American dumb-bell plan. At each end (of an area that can be the size of Liechtenstein) there is a major store (House of Fraser, Debenhams) with other big retailers equally spaced between them (Marks and Spencer, Bentalls). This arrangement keeps us moving. The soaring ceiling heights, the glass-sided moving staircases, the clear bubble lifts bobbing up and down the atrium, the movement of water and the sound of music all conspire to keep us edging our way forwards through the galleries of shops. There are not many places to sit or lean or rest the carrier bags without spending money on at least a cup of coffee, and there are the ever-present security guards (blue shirts reminiscent of American cops) wired up to some Mall Control Centre and,

doubtless, schooled in advanced techniques of: crowds, management of; individuals, eviction of; riots, containing the same. Just in case some crazed consumers feel like running amok American-style, or just lying on the marble floor and kicking their legs in the air from the sheer *overwhelmingness* of it all.

Piped music and uniform tills: environmental shopping conditioning courtesy of the Good Old US of A.

There's an element of control too in the colours used in the mall: soothing pastels and greenery for movement contrasting with the arresting colours of the food court outlets. Stop and graze colours. Stop for Chicken & Ribs, Crêpes & Ice-Cream, Pasta & Pizza.

And there's more. Mall customers are next in line to be led by the nose. Marketing Aromatics, part of the Behavioural Dynamics Company, has developed a range of whiffs to help us get into the spending mode. There's a fresh leather smell for car showrooms, Oriental spiciness for the travel agency and the encouraging smell of just-out-of-the-oven-French-stick for supermarkets. Simply peel one off and wait for the punters to come in smiling. Big companies have decided to be identified by smell. The official corporate fragrance of the Body Shop is dewberry. It's only a matter of time before your psycho-physiological response to the smell of feet takes you, credit card in hand, to any one – or all – of Lakeside's fourteen shoe shops.

So, in the whole scheme of things, should we be pleased or 'mall-content' that the Americans have given us their shopping-centre culture?

The anti lobby says no more malls because of the effect they have on high street shops at the heart of neighbouring towns. And it's not just the shops that go to the wall, it's kids with spray paint when a 'downtown' area gets boarded up, run down and generally begins to look like the opening sequence of *Hill Street Blues*.

American cities have long experienced what is known as 'the donut effect', where outer urban areas become prosperous (and sugary) while the centre turns into a big empty hole. Ross Davies of the Oxford Institute of Retail Management puts it bluntly:

> If the overall process of decentralisation continues at the same
> pace as in recent years, then we are likely to see the fragmentation
> of our cities on an unprecedented scale.

There certainly is tough competition between the town centre and the out-of-town mall. To ensure success the mall people must secure one or two big prestigious retailers or the other littler fish won't follow. They offer money if necessary. It was rumoured, though never proved, that the developers responsible for a new mall in the north of England gave one retailing company an £8 million cash inducement to sign up for a store.

Certainly nobody wants the building of a glittering mall to be at the cost of the hundreds of vacant premises, shops holding 'back-to-the-wall' closing-down sales and cheap-jack temporary stores which characterise many of the poorer American downtown areas. We'd prefer, say the anti-mall lobby, that our towns were commercially viable, lived in (as French city centres often are), full of people in the evening and, therefore, less hostile, dirty and crime-ridden.

Mall supporters say yes, let's build, American-style, and see what high-quality, super-clean malls can do to revitalise the image of some of our cities. After all, it worked a treat in Baltimore. The handsome steel-and-glass Harborplace shopping mall, crammed with shops and restaurants, is the city's pride and joy. It replaced the rotting wharves and derelict warehouses that lined the waterfront until the 1980s. The mall stands now at the centre of several tourist attractions and is a sympathetic and popular place for daytime and night-time visitors. In Britain mall supporters quote the Princes Square development in Glasgow, one of several key buildings that helped the city shake off its reputation as a weary, drunken, post-industrial metropolis with a great past but not much of a future.

And let the cultural snobs go hang, say mall enthusiasts. Why not put art and commerce back together again? Isn't that what has made a success of the revamped Liverpool Docks, where shopping, museums and the new Tate Gallery are cheek by jowl? It's a shame that Terry Farrell's design for a revamped South Bank including an up-market shopping centre had to be shelved. We want to reverse the British tendency to house artistic activity in special ghettos where it becomes inaccessible and forbidding. In the words of Philip Dodd of the *New Statesman*:

> This separation of culture and commerce is a long-standing
> British trait – culture has withdrawn from human life.

Let's have malls then, but ones which include libraries, galleries and spaces for performance. Let them be more individual, let them be designed by the best architects and let them sink the pastiche steamboat. Then we'd all be happy.

I'VE SEEN THE FUTURE … AND IT'S JUST YOUR SIZE

The shape of shops to come

'At any hour of the night or day you can go shopping at Macy's.' This startling claim was made by Don Hewitt, executive producer on the American TV news show *60 Minutes*. Don is now creative consultant on the home shopping cable TV channel called TV Macy's (TVM), which will be available on Channel 34 from autumn 1994. Telly shopping, the Americans say, is just 'keeping away from the Joneses'.

If you live on Long Island in the New York suburbs, for example, you have three home shopping channels to choose from, twenty-four hours a day. There's no membership fee, you just call and give your name and details and wait to be given a personal account number. You can pay by credit card, cheque, money order … just about anything except milk-bottle tops. If you're deaf, don't worry. The companies will give you a special terminal to print out your orders, so just sit back and watch.

Shopping channels are 'a department store in your living room'. They have live models showing you, in glorious 3D, the shape of that jacket or how to use that fly-fishing rod, and they have a snappy way of selling:

(Above) Striking lucky:
once, bowling alleys were
dives for undesirables.
Now, thanks to major
sponsors, bowling has re-
emerged as a respectable
family activity.

(Right) Mad dogs and
Englishmen: the midday
sun becomes the shoot out
at high noon.

(Left) Stars and stripes:
The Gap gets patriotic in
the name of fashion.

(Below) Burberry man sets
foot in Lillywhite's.

Item: a 14-carat gold magic herringbone chain. This lovely chain is
20 inches long, it weighs 17.24 grams and is 3/16ths inches wide.
The retail value in your downtown jewellery store is $831.66. But
here on Home Shopping Channel it's yours for just $295.30.
And wait. Special today on HSC is a blow-out price of an amazing
$254.75. But, ladies and gentlemen, you have only five minutes
to take advantage of this offer …

All this while a number counter is rolling in the corner of the screen to
show how many items have been sold, with a final 'All Sold Out at this
Price' announcement to make hesitant buyers feel as though they've
missed something.

Some shopping channels are run like game shows. Shoppers phone in,
discuss their purchases, their presents for the family, the wheel of fortune is
turned, maybe a woman from Georgia wins $600 worth of credit …

Macy's knows the extent of the telly shopping market, currently worth $2
billion. QVC, the largest shopping channel, has forty-four million
subscribers. Sak's Fifth Avenue, a rival department store to Macy's, sold
$570,000 worth of goods on the first day of its being featured on QVC.

The latest hot-selling items available on shopping channels in the United
States are bits of amber with mosquitoes preserved in them, which can be
worn round the neck. These souvenirs of *Jurassic Park* cannot be
guaranteed to start a new race of dinosaurs but, at $39.50, who's
complaining?

In Britain home shopping has been looming for a generation, but never
properly launched. When the Prestel system flopped, people said it was
because you could walk to the shop more quickly than accessing the page.
Richard Hyman of Verdict, the research company to the retail trade, says
that home shopping is one area where the Americans and the British really
show their differences as consumers. Recession and technical difficulties
aside, he says that the slow start to home shopping in Britain is to do with
the distribution of population. We are, after all, pretty tightly packed into
a landscape that would fit easily into a medium-sized American state.
Generally, real shops, where we can touch and examine the goods, are
accessible. In Britain public transport mostly still works, so that even
people without cars can find their way to shopping centres. In the United
States, the elderly, often referred to as 'shut-ins', do not have such an easy
time and they make up a significant proportion of the telly shopping

audience. In France, where the Minitel home shopping system is established (and very dull compared to the United States equivalent), French telecommunications invested heavily at first in a way that, apparently, British Telecom is unwilling to do.

One kind of compromise for the British shopper which puts us more on American lines has been worked out by Joe Pannu, chairman of the Original Video Catalogue Company. He has produced a fashion catalogue on video which is aimed at 20–45-year-olds. Initially, 100,000 people will receive the tape, which he hopes will be 'a bit more glamorous' than a regular book-style catalogue and give the mail-order customer a proper three-dimensional idea of what the clothes look like. In years to come Pannu plans to launch the catalogue elsewhere in Europe, Australia, Japan and (here comes the boomerang) the United States … mail order goes *global*.

A much more immediate influence from the USA is the 'silent enemy', the traditional retailer's nightmare: the Warehouse Club. WCs like Price Club, Costco and Sam's are the fastest-growing retailing sector in America, with sales of nearly $30 billion annually. Punters pay a membership fee ($25–30) that gives them access to the club's gigantic warehouses, which are three or four times the size of a big Sainsbury's, vast hangars full of basic weekly provisions. The costs are cut because of a terrifically

Whoever Has Most Things When He Dies Wins.

AMERICAN T-SHIRT SLOGAN

high turnover and a low-cost, factory-style environment. Costco has acquired two sites in Britain and another, unnamed, company has taken two more, while Littlewoods, the British mail-order company, has announced its intention to get into bed with Price Club, the big warehouse name in Canada, to bring their product idea across the Atlantic.

Along the same lines, watch out for the arrival from across the water of McArthur/Glen, whose stock-in-trade is what is known and loved in the USA as the 'manufacturers' outlet' or 'factory outlet' centre. Here is where end-of-lines, seconds, production over-runs and liquidation stock find a willing market at up to 40 per cent below regular retail prices.

We can glimpse here the beginning of a new division in retail society: poorer people shop in warehouses/factories, while rich people shop in service-intensive stores that are design-led.

COMING SOON … much older shop assistants. Demographic trends – which are clearly towards an ageing population – make this inevitable on

(Main pic) The essential
movie accessory – sweet or
salty 'sound crackle'.

(Inset) Plastic orange
cartons with needle straws
are a thing of the past in
the multiscreen cinema.
Now, if there's no
popcorn, no sweets, no
chocolate chip ice cream,
there's no party.

both sides of the Atlantic but, in common with some US companies, Tesco and B&Q have already started actively to recruit older people on the basis that they are more reliable, conscientious and more in tune with the idea of serving the customer.

COMING SOON ... the rise of the grey pound. In the United States the American Association of Retired Persons is a major consumer force. The babyboomers who have had it their own way since the 1960s will, in their dotage, be shaping the shopping of the future. Predictions are that this will be more design-conscious, more specialised and, in the middle-class sector, less frantic than in recent years.

The Americans have persuaded us, I think, that with ever more niche selling, you simply can't have *too many* shops. There isn't a place in the universe that wouldn't benefit from a retail outlet, no time of day (including Sunday) when a little retail therapy doesn't make the world look brighter. A trip to the Planet Hollywood theme restaurant in London is nothing without the souvenir: the embroidered T-shirt £14.99; the sports watch £13.99; the reversible jacket £199.99; the gorilla £12.99. And OK, railway stations, museums, art galleries, libraries (where more bookshops would be an excellent idea) are legitimately in the retail arena but – hospitals?

> I found niche retailing raging at the Sheffield Hallamshire Hospital.
> The entrance hall (or should one call it the shopping village?) is crowded
> out with bookstalls, gift shops, flower stalls. Indeed, in this bonanza
> of retailing activity the appearance of an actual patient, ashen-faced in his
> wheelchair, strikes one as a little thoughtless, like the unwanted spectre
> at the feast. It is hard to remember that this is a place of healing.
> Fiona MacCarthy, *The Guardian*, 1989

Who are we with in the end? Are we with expansionist Dan Quayle, the former United States vice-president, who, with famous clarity, said that far from there being too many shops and a saturated market there was:

> Er, a lot of space. It's finite – well, no, some people think it's infinite in fact.
> There's a lot of uncharted waters. Well, anyway, we're going to go for it.

Or are we with that older American statesman, Adlai Stevenson, who asked:

> With the supermarket as our temple and the singing commercial as
> our litany, are we likely to fire the world with an irresistible
> vision of America's exalted purposes and inspiring way of life?

The chequered shirt

The boys said Saturday night would be somethin' else. Worth waitin' and workin' the week for. And there, sure enough, parked up outside the bar was Reb's red customised van – crossed Confederate rifles painted on the front, Arizona landscape and the Alamo on each shiny flank.

Even from this distance we could hear the band, Buntline Special, and make out the yearning lyrics of a Patsy Cline classic.

Inside, the bar was packed with men: representatives of every kind of cowpoke, hobo, lawman, saddletramp, drifter, gunslinger and regular cowboy that ever spat in the dust of the Ol' Wild West. Mean lookin' men, some of them – grizzly and unshaven with sweaty shirts and leather chaps worn thin. Some of the guys *had* washed up, it being Saturday an' all. They'd cleaned the trail dirt out of their ears and were on parade, clean and gleaming as a marshal's badge.

There was Slim – saloon slicker in a bootlace tie fastened with a sapphire clip, the points of his shirt finished with a pair of silver chevrons. At his waist two guns in a rig (we don't say holster in the real West) that was tied to his leg with a leather thong. In a hoarse whisper, against the music, he told me he used to be an Indian. I believed him. Missing one or two teeth himself, he'd made up for it with a couple of wild critter's teeth on a choker round his neck. What were they? Coyote? 'Gator? BUFFALO?

Billy Montana was all in black, the arms of his silky shirt arrested with bands of leather and silver. A big dark hat shadowed his face. There was Silver Fox, Sundance Kid, Eagle, Doc, Buck Jones, Chester and Lonely in

These people are simple farmers, people of the land, the common clay of the New West. You know – morons.

MEL BROOKS,
BLAZING SADDLES, 1974

Now you can wear
your spurs with pride,
even if you don't come
from Tottenham.

45

a battered top hat (nobody talks to him). There was Reb practising his quick draw and Buffalo Bill dancing with a pretty saloon girl, grinning through his goatee beard and moustache. Laughing Water, a homely, cheerful Indian squaw, was leading the ladies in some 'line dancing' (remember the Shadows?) while Kath on stage in rhinestone-encrusted blue jeans belted it out: 'I Fall to Pieces' …

And where, in the name of Sitting Bull, are we? Not Deadwood, South Dakota, not Dodge City, Kansas, not even Surrey with the Fringe on Top. This is the Crosby Head pub next to the fire station on Old Street roundabout in the City of London. Cowboy Bluff, you could call it.

And you can bet your boots that tonight all over Britain, from the Crosby Head to the Firth of Forth, in other bars, at barbecues and on campsites, other cowboys and girls, most of whom will never see the sky over the Oregon Trail, are living out this same Saturday night fever, propping up the unflaggingly popular myth of the Old Wild West.

> *It's sort of like the cavalry coming to the rescue.*
>
> GENERAL COLIN POWELL,
> EXPLAINING THE
> AMERICAN MISSION IN SOMALIA

Take Reb (real name Dennis). Reb's in leather chaps made at home out of a pair of welding overalls. He says he hasn't washed his cowboy shirt for six years and that if anyone were so much as to *breathe* on it, it would fall to shreds. He wears a stetson with a fully functional grease band and a low-slung gun that fires blanks and cost him £217. Reb doesn't approve of 'plastic' or 'Hollywood' cowboys, as he calls them, ones who dress in fringes and finery like Roy Rodgers. He's from the play-and-sleep-rough-like-the-real-men-did school of modern cowboys.

But Reb isn't just *any* saddletramp. His adopted character is one of the Regulators, a band of men who played their part in the story of the West. They were a private army of misfits who were hired by ranchers during the range wars to protect them and their property. Some had been Confederate soldiers and had lost their homes and livelihoods and women. All the Regulators, and the other cowboy groups – the Frontiersmen, Westerners, Virginians, Texas Rangers, Trappers (and the Crinoline Cavalry) – know who they are and something about the forty years of extraordinary American history that spawned the cowboy culture. Among Reb's cowboy cups is one for Fastest Draw and, not surprisingly, one for Most Authentic Cowboy.

Reb says that everyone, including his girlfriend, calls him Reb now. It started seven years ago when he saw a group of urban cowboys in a pub on

Jamaica Road. Reb's a truck driver by trade, a 'plain person', he says, who is someone special at the weekend. Though there were some teething troubles with the cowboy kit (wearing new boots and spurs he fell down the stairs of a double-decker – more *Wayne's World* than John Wayne's world), now he says he *is* Reb. Reb walks differently from Dennis, he feels different.

> It's not a fantasy. It's as though I was born a cowboy. In the fast draw competitions I'm quick because I think to myself: 'This is real. These are real bullets.' I love dressing like this. It's only my mother who doesn't like it. When I go to her house she asks me if anyone saw me come in.

Reb and the others can't say exactly what attracts them to the Wild West. They like the clothes, the charity fund-raising. 'We hold up buses with our guns firing and demand money. Once we did a raid on a police station.' They like the companionship. But perhaps at the heart of it is a late twentieth-century longing for a world in which the individual had control (and a real gun). During the 1849 Gold Rush, the Civil War, the Plains Indian wars and afterwards, pioneers shaped their own destiny and took their chances against attackers, swindlers, rustlers and freezing/scorching, crop-destroying weather.

In the West (and the early black and white cowboy films that paid it tribute) good and bad were easier to distinguish than they are now. In the West there was a satisfying reliance on rough justice – an acceptance that vigilantes and professional gunmen would give the Sheriff a hand, whether he liked it or not, and do 'what a man's gotta do'. Lawbreakers like Jesse and Frank James, Butch Cassidy and Josey Wales

This may be Dodge City, but Wyatt is in town.
A MARINE SPOKESMAN IN MOGADISHU

were interpreted as social rebels and folk heroes. In the cult of the outlaw a man could do wrong but for the right reason (protecting the little folks against banks and railroads and smart-talking honchos from back East) and get away with it.

And how much more romantic the cowboy (whose at-home-on-the-range, rugged good looks are still selling Marlboro cigarettes) than the posse of lawyers, government representatives, railway officials and tax collectors who followed him out West.

The myth of the Wild West was made, with typically American haste, just as the last moments of the real-life story were being played out. In 1890 at the Battle of Wounded Knee, 300 Sioux were massacred by the

The call of the wild: the regulators
gather for a pow-wow in Old Street.

army; resistance to white expansion in the West was over. In 1899 the last stage-coach robbery took place (perpetrated by a woman). Yet by 1905, just a few years later, the Antiquities Act had been passed to protect the artefacts of what was already the Old Wild West – the giant cacti, missions and ancient Indian buildings. The American Bison Society were campaigning to save the buffalo from extinction and the Apache chief, Geronimo, had become a tourist attraction and appeared at the inauguration of Theodore Roosevelt.

As early as 1883 – only two years after the gunfight at the OK Corral took place and made Wyatt Earp a national figure – a former Indian scout called William Frederick Cody organised his first Wild West Show. Buffalo Bill, as he was known, had earned a living supplying buffalo meat to the railway gangs who, in their heyday, were laying track at the rate of five miles a day. When the railroad was built, he took up show business. His circus, which included the sharp-shooting Annie Oakley, came to England where Queen Victoria saw it twice. Grainy pictures of Bill's European tour show him with several fully kitted real Indians sitting in a gondola in Venice.

At the Crosby Head, our Buffalo Bill *manqué* seems not to mind imitating a man who was *himself* only dressing the part. Show business is a legitimate Western trade. Bill (real name Peter), like Reb, has done his research:

> When Bill's father died from a knife wound, young Bill had to look
> after the family. He was a great rider – held the record for distance
> covered on horseback in one day – couple of hundred miles, I think.
> He was tall and liked women and he was good at business, had two
> or three ranches until he boozed it all away. He ended up bankrupt
> and sold the circus to Barnum and Bailey.

Pete's ambition is to open a Wild West hotel where all the guests are in costume and in character – their cars and campers and any reminder of the late twentieth century safely out of sight. He reckons the cowboy thing is growing.

If Bill/Pete is right he can thank the band of film and music makers who have kept cowboys alive in our imaginations long after they should have hung up their spurs for the last time. Film makers in particular have been skilled at adapting the stories of the Wild West to the cultural and political climate of the times. In the silent movie it was enough to round up the usual suspects: the gambler, the lawman, the Mexican bandit, the dignified outlaw and the down-home girl who redeems and loves him. After (a) catching his sliding drink from the end of the bar, (b) galloping across some impressive scenery, and (c) killing a man in a black hat or, better still, one who wears an eye patch, our rufty, tufty hero is home and dry.

By the time the depressing 1930s had arrived audiences didn't want to be reminded of the dusty struggle to win the West. They'd prefer a cheerful musical, thank you very much. But the Second World War meant that cowboys (and soldiers in cavalry uniform) could be used in thinly veiled endorsements of the patriotic message. Later on the makers of Westerns approached their subject more subtly. Moral judgements about alienated gunfighters and the rights of Native Americans (as they became known) were finely balanced with the entertainment values of the films. *The Wild Bunch* (1969), in which a band of outlaws confront a Mexican dictator who has killed one of their number, is clearly informed by the political uncertainty over America's war in Vietnam. *Dances with Wolves* (1991) was a lament for lost innocence and the white man's broken bond with nature. Appropriate enough in an age of environmental awareness.

For Reb and Bill who collect Westerns, from early black and whites through John Ford to *The Unforgiven*, the best recent cowboy movies have been *Young Guns* parts I and II.

'West of the Mississippi, North of the Rio Grande' is a new exhibition which pays tribute to the Western at MOMI, the Museum of the Moving Image in London.

> Displays take a look at the origin of the cowboy and how he entered
> the movies. There's a reconstruction of a Western saloon … a
> diorama projection of selected spectacular outdoor sequences …
> live acts accompany the exhibition …

The other regular shot in the arm for cowboy culture, and its constant accompaniment, is country music. Flicking through Reb's copy of *Southern Country* magazine, which lists hundreds of country bands, fixtures, dance classes, cowboy outfitters, cowboy holidays, you suddenly realise that there's a huge American-inspired sub-culture around country music which is like a hidden iceberg. At its tip in Britain there are a few TV shows and Radio 2's specialist country music programmes, but underneath there's a massive potential audience which is being poorly served.

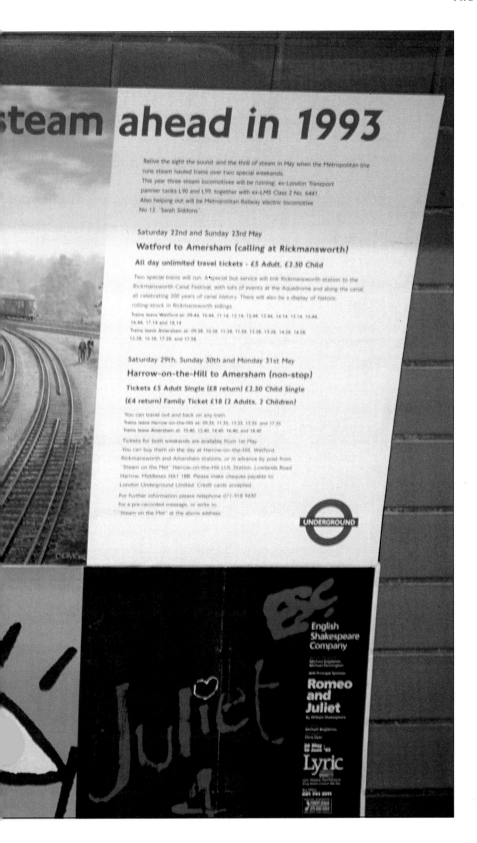

steam ahead in 1993

Relive the sight the sound, and the thrill of steam in May when the Metropolitan line runs steam hauled trains over two special weekends.

This year three steam locomotives will be running: ex-London Transport pannier tanks L90 and L99, together with ex-LMS Class 2 No. 6441

Also helping out will be Metropolitan Railway electric locomotive No 12. 'Sarah Siddons'.

Saturday 22nd and Sunday 23rd May

Watford to Amersham (calling at Rickmansworth)

All day unlimited travel tickets - £5 Adult, £2.50 Child

Two special trains will run. A special bus service will link Rickmansworth station to the Rickmansworth Canal Festival, with lots of events at the Aquadrome and along the canal, all celebrating 200 years of canal history. There will also be a display of historic rolling-stock in Rickmansworth sidings

Trains leave Watford at: 09.44, 10.44, 11.14, 12.14, 13.44, 13.44, 14.14, 15.14, 15.44, 16.44, 17.14 and 18.14

Trains leave Amersham at: 09.58, 10.28, 11.28, 11.58, 13.08, 13.58, 14.28, 14.58, 15.58, 16.28, 17.28, and 17.58

Saturday 29th, Sunday 30th and Monday 31st May

Harrow-on-the-Hill to Amersham (non-stop)

Tickets £5 Adult Single (£8 return) £2.50 Child Single (£4 return) Family Ticket £18 (2 Adults, 2 Children)

You can travel out and back on any train.

Trains leave Harrow-on-the-Hill at: 09.55, 11.55, 13.55, 15.55, and 17.55

Trains leave Amersham at: 10.40, 12.40, 14.40, 16.40, and 18.40

Tickets for both weekends are available from 1st May.

You can buy them on the day at Harrow-on-the-Hill, Watford, Rickmansworth and Amersham stations, or in advance by post from 'Steam on the Met' Harrow-on-the-Hill L.U.R. Station, Lowlands Road Harrow, Middlesex HA1 3BB. Please make cheques payable to London Underground Limited. Credit cards accepted.

For further information please telephone 071-918 9430 for a pre-recorded message, or write to 'Steam on the Met' at the above address.

UNDERGROUND

English Shakespeare Company

Romeo and Juliet

By William Shakespeare

Lyric

Catching the last west-bound train.

In America, where for so long rockabilly music was poor people's entertainment, country is now king. It has doubled its share of record sales in the United States since 1990, there are 2,500 country radio stations nationwide and a country music cable TV station. The solo debut album by Wynona Judd, who used to sing with her mum as The Judds, sold a million copies within six days. Chubby Garth Brooks, country music's biggest superstar, can outsell Michael Jackson despite his terrible shirts and having, as one newspaper called it, 'excess longitude under the chin'. Record executives, dismayed by the narrow popularity of rap and grunge, are busy trying to sign country artists who can cross over from the achy-breaky, hurtin' and hopin' and copin' world of old-fashioned country into the new realm of country rock.

At the Crosby Head the cowboys like the old tunes best. Not for them the new wave of American country songs which challenge cowboy conservatism and the redneck tendency. Garth Brooks's recent album *The Chase*, had the megastar preaching lyrically about tolerance in a song called 'We Shall Be Free':

> When this world's big enough for all different views
> When we can worship from our own kind of pew
> Then we shall be free.

Liberalism? Or a shrewd nod in the direction of the gay community, who are country music's newest and keenest fans?

Kath and the Buntline Special band may one day be caught up in the British explosion of country music and a new era of slick videos, stage shows, merchandise and fanzines. Until then it's Patsy Cline, who's another gay icon on both sides of the Atlantic (and an archetypal United States star who was born in poverty, had a hard time, a car crash, a husband who beat her up and, finally, died in an aeroplane accident). While Kath sings Patsy in that light, pure, lilting voice, the cowboys dream of rodeo, the open range, a fast gun and a faithful woman.

Have you been to Milton Keynes?

America's most well-known gift to Milton Keynes is that much lampooned collection of concrete cows that you can see from the train; a static herd that became a symbol of a city that some said was lifeless itself. They were the work of the US sculptress Liz Leyh, the city's first artist-in-residence, and I have no doubt that in the dark days of the worst Milton Keynes jokes ('Did you know that man is the only animal that can experience boredom?' … 'I know, I've been to Milton Keynes') that the head of the Development Corporation would willingly have paid for them to be taken away to some concrete abattoir or drowned in their concrete overcoats.

But the American influence in Milton Keynes goes back further than this. The birth of the city was trumpeted in full American style with publicists and PR men storming over the hill like the cavalry. Milton Keynes wasn't so much presented to the world as a jolly good idea as *launched* like a new model Ford. The plans were revealed at the Design Centre in London in 1968. The whole place was carpeted with bright green Astroturf and dotted with life-size stuffed sheep. Against a theatrically painted backdrop of rural England and blue skies rose a huge white model of the city of the future. From Deptford to Des Moines everyone suddenly knew about Milton Keynes. The magazines which ran features on the new city stacked up higher than its tallest proposed building.

The corporation did the corporate thing: it had a glossy brochure, *New City*, it had an HQ, it handled promotion, lobbied politicians, wooed investors and … had a vision of a city that celebrated the American, but not very English, virtues of convenience, efficiency, amenity, opportunity

Why does Milton Keynes remind me of Gertrude Stein's remark about Oakland in California, saying that there is no 'there' there?

ANONYMOUS

Love it or hate it, Milton Keynes is uniquely American. To many, it is the lifestyle and not the architecture that provides the attraction.

and imagination. What it had in mind was The Good Life in which poor, benighted city-dwellers (represented in the corporate magazine by the Reynolds family, who lived in Brixton and had a tin bath on the outside wall of their Victorian terrace) could overspill into a city which was green and open.

It would be egalitarian. The charcoal smoke from the barbecues of workers and bosses would mingle at Sunday lunchtime. Nobody would need more than fifteen minutes to get to work. Everyone could go home to lunch, or go shopping, or jogging. Milton Keynes wasn't ever going to be like Bristol or York or Edinburgh … it was going to be a lot easier to park.

The city was built, of course, on the American-style system of grid roads (known in MK as H-roads and V-roads – win a toaster if you automatically know that this means horizontal and vertical). Coast to coast, American towns had been planned on the grid system since the beginning. And for a number of different reasons.

In America in the early days of settlement, they used the grid system as the most convenient way of parcelling out land for development. The idealistic city fathers hoped that it was egalitarian too by inviting (as it did at first) easy, small-purchase entry into the urban land market. Later this 'colonial' grid arrangement worked in the interests of those not so dedicated to equality. In nineteenth-century Washington DC, for example, the large dignified upper-class blocks concealed a back grid of alley ghettos for poor, black, servant families.

In Salt Lake City Joseph Smith and his followers in the Church of Jesus Christ of the Latter-Day Saints laid out a city on the grid system because that is what they believed God wanted them to do. The ideal Mormon scheme was called the Plat of the City of Zion: houses formed squares of orderly settlement, each one leased to the church, in a pattern which could be replicated endlessly. It was to be the perfect place for the Second Coming.

But it wasn't until the twentieth century that America produced grid suburbs on a really awesome scale. Not for nothing is Los Angeles referred to as nineteen suburbs in search of a city. By the 1950s, thirty million Americans lived in the vast suburbs around Chicago – each of them routinely starting off in a $15,000 house with three bedrooms, two bathrooms, a living-room/diner (maybe split-level) with a picture window and, outside, a patch of lawn, a garage and a mail-box. New tools and methods of prefabricating buildings made these suburbs astonishingly quick and easy to construct. On Long Island, Abraham Levitt turned land on which he had grown potatoes into a suburb for 100,000 people. In Levittown there was only one style of house but it came in five varieties of colour and finish. Families would use these homes as the first rung on the ladder, with the idea that, as they prospered, they would move to a bigger house in another suburb, and then to a bigger house still …

With four walk-in closets to walk in. Three bushes, two shrubs and one tree, The Suburbs are good for the children But no place for grown-ups to be.

JUDITH VIORST,
'ITS HARD TO BE HIP OVER THIRTY'

From America we got the idea that suburbia was about conformity on a frightening scale. American developments were not planned overall by any public authority. The builder merely had to follow a set of regulations about lot size, yard size, the distance of the building from the road and so on. Hence what they built tended to be mind-numbingly monotonous.

From the 1950s suburbia was regarded as home to that ideal, happy, American, Kellogg's-cornflake-eating family. *He* commutes in a grey flannel suit, an aspiring soldier in a large corporation where the chain of command is not unlike that of the armed forces. *She* stays at home, taking delivery of babies and consumer durables. No wonder Arthur Miller found such rich and painful material in the domestic life of Middle America. No wonder the Stepford Wives are such a haunting image.

Milton Keynes is certainly a suburb, much more sub than urb, with little or no pretensions to being a city (in so far as cities are complex, centrally focused seats of power) in anything but name. In style it does owe something to those post-war American suburbs, but there is an equal debt to the Garden City tradition pioneered at the turn of the century by Ebenezer Howard. Howard had spent time in Chicago and had seen the city grow unchecked – a dense, aggressive centre giving way to an outer sprawl with a more ragged fringe beyond that … a fringe that touched the edges of the next town. Conurbation, he called it.

The Garden City idea was to combine 'all the advantages of the most active and energetic town life with the beauty and delight of the country'. The city would be planned to a specific size once a private company had acquired the land. It would be surrounded by an unassailable green belt of land. In the United States the whole idea was a spectacular failure.

Living well: the LA gym concept comes to Milton Keynes.

Anything but outright, individual commercial ownership was anathema. And controls on land use – it just sounded a bit too much like some pinko, socialist ideal.

But in Milton Keynes they've pulled it off. The planners had a vision of a Garden City, took a measure of control and then, between the grids as it were, offered hundreds of pockets of opportunity to private development. The thing is that Milton Keynes does feel like a place that's very American in its aspirations. Spread over 34 square miles it behaves as though space were no problem. Its boulevards are an American, not a French, import. What's more it's proud of being modern and would sympathise with Le Corbusier's Modernist abhorrence of old cities where the layout has been 'dictated by the pack donkey'. Corbusier's view was that: 'Man walks in a straight line because he has a goal and knows where he is going.' Milton Keynes is not a city for meandering.

There's something frank and classless about Milton Keynes: in common with the United States it is not shackled to historical imperatives about how things ought to be. Milton Keynes is not for people who value the quaint, mystical and old. Its values are bold, rational, progressive and materialist. It flies in the face of the kind of old world snobbery that prompted *Harpers & Queen* to attack the city as 'unbearably new and depressingly desolate'. It faced, after 20 years, the same glib criticism that the United States faced after 200 – no culture, no antiquity, no definable heart.

Yet, like America, it delivers what a lot of people regard as The Good Life, a life worth pioneering for. In the words of Sir Henry Chilver, chairman of the Milton Keynes Development Corporation during the 1980s:

> People came with very real expectations – which were fulfilled – that
> you could, almost by dint of personal and family enterprise, get involved
> in a city of enormously high quality. The environment was excellent,
> there were opportunities for starting afresh. Your children went to
> new schools. The streets were clean and wide open.

The local Tory MP Bill Benyon described the people of Milton Keynes as 'apolitical. They are classless. They are the new Briton.' Mrs Thatcher, who has done for American values in Britain what Wrigley's did for gum, loved Milton Keynes, her 'city of entrepreneurs', where the first principle was opportunity and freedom of choice. Once the Development Corporation had been knocked into shape and encouraged to take a less interventionist role, her admiration was complete.

Here was a city in which car ownership was not merely expected but *welcomed*, with thousands of free parking spaces. (Early plans for a city monorail were abandoned in favour of the motor car.) Milton Keynes was where 55 per cent of houses (including Tudorbethan homes for those who chose them) were going to be in owner occupation; where many Japanese and ninety-eight American companies would set up shop; where the new De Montfort University taught business studies and computing; where there was even a new American campus-style private prison.

Let's spend a day, then, in England's most American city.

Limber up for the working day by jogging down the Trim Trail. A quick breakfast at home in one of Milton Keynes's California Collection houses. The California Collection got its glamorous name, I assume, from someone who has watched plenty of American TV. These houses are cross-breeds – all pillars and picture windows, double garages, ornamental gates and Georgian front doors. They're big. Big enough to accommodate the average comedy or soap opera set. Shows in which, for that past twenty-five years, someone has opened the front door to canned applause and said: 'Hi Honey, I'm ho-ome!' *Peyton Place? I Love Lucy? The Dick van Dyke Show? The Cosby Show? The Golden Girls?* These houses are versions of Southfork for people with normal-sized shoulders/incomes/families. Inside, they are that peculiarly American blend of fussy and bare.

In the car, on the tree-screened, uncongested roads, it takes less than fifteen minutes to get to work. (Where do people take their driving test? There are no hill starts, no unmarked crossroads and there's very little reason to change gear.) On the way you pass the Coca-Cola factory, a Tesco superstore in red brick with a clocktower – heritage architecture of the sort popular in the United States, and The Point, an American-owned ten-screen cinema, Britain's first multiplex. You notice that every screen but one is showing an American movie, including *Brain Dead: Total Mental Shutdown*, the story of a 1950s' bobbysoxer whose mother develops an insatiable craving for raw meat.

Your workplace has an atrium. It is light, relaxed and efficient and there's a little machine in the corner that dispenses paper cups and iced water. At lunchtime, corporate membership of the Living Well health club puts you in sweaty contact with several exercise machines – Cybex, Startrack, Stairmaster, Lifecycle and Powercise, all of them imported from the US. Maybe you're in training for the corporate games which Milton Keynes executives take very seriously. Your final fifteen-minute break is spent

(Above) Friendly but focussed: Milton Keynes Marketing has the city's future mapped out.

(Right) Chilly tropical heaven in MK? Indoor American ecology theories collide. Searing jungle heat turns to ice-cold air conditioning within three paces.

(Left) Frighteningly
clean: litter is alien to
Milton Keynes.

(Below) The California
collection: only the
weather rains on their
parade here.

sunning yourself in the tanning cabins known as Hawaii and Bahamas. On the way out, a small notice on the exit gate exhorts you to Have a Nice Day.

After work, whaddya want? Tenpin bowling at Super Bowl? A bout of Quasar (serious fun with a laser gun) in which you can run about in a dark maze wearing Dayglo body armour, 'shooting' the opposing team with killer beams of laser light? (Milton Keynes is the town that turned down the opportunity to give Luton Football Club a new home on the basis that it didn't want 'a hooligan problem'.)

Maybe a bite to eat at Houston's American-theme restaurant?

> Are you up the Houston's Challenge? Choose the Ultimate Main Course – ribs, wings, jambalaya, beans, beef chilli, chicken enchilada and rice, OR Bust a Gut on a 16 oz rump steak served with fries and stir fry vegetables.

Or late shopping at the mall, though you'll have to hurry because although this thoroughfare is also the very centre of town it's locked after shopping hours and on Sunday. Sadly, if you want to see a play or hear a classical music concert you'll have to go elsewhere. MK is more a venue for popular music, with big American stars such as Michael Jackson and Bruce Springsteen playing to huge audiences in the city.

In Milton Keynes life is convenient. There's an American expectation that work and family life can mesh easily together and be fun. Lots for the third agers (elderly) to do, plenty of access for disabled people, a nicely rounded all-denominations-welcome ecumenical church and picturesque corners like Pennylands Boat Station development alongside the canal: 'We use this shot for our lifestyle brochures.'

So would a seasoned city-dweller want to live in this wide, low US-style, reasonable city among ten million trees? I think Terence Bendixson, author of the book *Milton Keynes: Image and Reality*, hit home when he said: 'The rational in us admires its logic. The romantic in us fears its order.'

Why won't Elvis die?

America is unmatched in its production of icons. Nowhere can a star shine more brightly, epitomise a whole generation, crash through more superlatives and attract more attention from passionate fans, blood-letting journalists, hip academics, loony tunes, religious revivalists and hucksters just bent on making a buck on anybody's back. When James Dean's wrecked Porsche was put on display in Los Angeles after the fatal accident, 800,000 Americans queued up to see it. Some paid extra to sit in what was left of the seat where Dean died. Now *that's* iconolatry.

The moment I stepped off the plane at Memphis a strange and wonderful feeling came over me. It's hard to describe, but I know what caused it: the thought of being a few miles from Elvis.

A FAN'S STORY
IN ELVIS MONTHLY, 1965

Whom the gods love die young-ish. And all the world loves that first wave of dead stars, Americans who between 1953 and 1977 squandered their talent in front-page disaster deaths – deaths that were before their time: Hank Williams (plane crash, 1953); James Dean (car crash, 1956); Buddy Holly and Richie Valens (plane crash, 1959); Eddie Cochran (car crash, 1960; Gene Vincent survived but his career didn't); Marilyn Monroe (allegedly an overdose, 1962), Patsy Cline (plane crash, 1963); Otis Redding (plane crash, 1967).

But the greatest, the most exciting, frightening and influential icon was Elvis Presley, who died on 16 August 1977, slumped on a lavatory deep in the excesses of the Graceland mansion. A man who redefined popular culture and was its most perfect martyr.

The first test of a genuine blue-chip American icon is its ability to endure. Since Elvis's death, 'the best career move he could have made', he's been bigger, more bizarre, more prolific and *richer* than he ever was during his

Elvis lives. For many
Brits, he will always be the
King of America.

lifetime. In 1979, two years after his death, the Presley estate's annual income was a mere $1 million. Elvis did not even receive royalties from the vast majority of his recordings. These went to RCA, his record company, which had bought perpetual rights to 700 tracks (including the best of the 1950s stuff – 'Hound Dog', 'Jailhouse Rock', 'Return to Sender') from Elvis's manager and mentor, Colonel Tom Parker, in 1973 for a lump-sum of $5.4 million.

But in the early '80s, his image was relaunched and his name and likeness protected from commercial abuse by a new United States law, the Personal Rights Protection Act, which was pioneered by Roger Richman – attorney to such dead greats as Marilyn Monroe and Sigmund Freud. Priscilla, Elvis's estranged wife, came back into the fold, formed Elvis Presley Enterprises and spent $500,000 on Graceland before opening it to the public in 1982. She got her money back in thirty-eight days. By investing in hundreds of exhibits, including Elvis's cars, his clothes and all of his 340 gold discs, she transformed the man into a brand. That brand now grosses $15 million a year. With an admission price of $16, Graceland attracts more visitors than any other building in America except the White House. Apparently more people visit Elvis's grave in the Meditation Garden at Graceland (catching a glimpse of his mother's pink Cadillac in the car port) than visit the grave of President Kennedy.

Owning the rights to the image of Elvis is like having a licence to print money. Sixteen years after his death he still ranks among the world's top ten entertainment moneymakers.

The interest in Elvis is unflagging on both sides of the Atlantic. In Britain record and video sales are still substantial. *For the Heart*, the most recent Presley release, a collection of love songs which came out for Valentine's Day, sold 250,000 copies. The official British Elvis Presley Fan Club has a membership of more than 20,000 with fifty branches nationwide. It runs a bi-monthly magazine, a summer festival at a holiday camp and regular trips to Elvis territory in Tennessee each January (His birthday) and August (for Death Week). This year, three tours were available – The Memorial, The Memorial with Memphis Extension and The Grand Memorial including Niagara Falls – up to £1,400 worth of closeness to the King.

Todd Slaughter, secretary of the British fan club since 1967 and leader of the Elvis Presley tours from 1972 onwards, met the King on several occasions and was there at Presley's last concert, six weeks before his death.

'He wasn't at all like showbusiness people. He seemed shy, insecure even.'
What about the excesses, the women?

> Graceland *was* full of women. But then there were fifteen blokes in
> Elvis's entourage who lived in that house – and plenty of girls
> who'd exchange sex with them for meeting Elvis Presley. I mean,
> performers do have big sexual appetites – even a turn in a working-
> man's club will pull every night, won't he? Giving everything
> on stage, naturally, they want something back at the end of it.
> But, for all the rumours, there haven't been too many 'I was laid
> by Elvis/He was a monster or a mouse in bed' stories in the papers.

The death of Elvis and the horrible way it happened was distressing to
British fans.

> They used to look at Elvis through rose-coloured glasses. I remember
> when Priscilla Presley got pregnant, many fans simply refused to believe
> that Elvis could *do* a thing like that.

They are purists. At fan club events there's very rarely an Elvis
impersonator, simply because no one comes close to delivering the
authentic Presley punch. 'The only exception, strangely,' says Todd, 'is
Freddy Starr, who is an Elvis nutcase. He did a whole evening with BBC
orchestra backing about seven years ago and he really was the business.'

Though official Elvis fans may be sniffy about impersonators, they are an
endless source of entertainment for the rest of us. Jonathan Ross, who
fancies himself as a bit of an early Elvis lookalike, has made television
programmes rounding up the hopefuls. Indeed, so many impersonators
exist that they are expected to audition and then register as acts that have
reached a minimum standard of competence. Why it is that British
impersonators tend to choose to copy the Elvis of Las Vegas, rather than
the young man, remains a mystery. Of course, the white and gold catsuit
with monster collar does help the audience recognise that it's Elvis you're
impersonating, and maybe the deep, wavering ballad-singing voice is easier
to practise in the bathroom mirror than the Jumping-Jack-Flashiness of
'Blue Suede Shoes'. Or perhaps it's just because we feel more comfortable
with a fading star than a rising one.

In the British press not a week passes without some reference to Elvis, a
new theory about his death, a 'sighting' in a car park in Wisconsin, an
allegation that a statue of Elvis has been found on Mars, or that he's
working as a pizza chef in Stevenage. The *Daily Sport*'s offer of a £2
million reward for anyone who can find Elvis, however, remains

(Above) Suspicious minds?
Kim Bridges sounds
spookily like the great
man himself.

(Right) Alive and
well in Streatham five
nights a week.

(Left) Elvis and the Antiques Roadshow: next to commemorative cups of the Queen are busts of the King.

(Below) Elvis lives on in Leicester. Todd Slaughter has taken thousands of Euro Elvis fans on the annual homage to Graceland.

unclaimed. Then there are the endless scrapings from the bottom of the barrel of personal recollection, like this one in the *Daily Mail*:

> According to Mary Jenkins, Elvis's cook for 14 years, the King liked nothing better at bedtime than two pieces of toast crammed with peanut butter and sliced banana and then fried in two sticks of butter. 'Oh, yeah, that was a lot of butter but Elvis wouldn't have it any other way.'

This year the acoustic guitar (a 1942 Martin D-18) that Elvis played on his 1954 recordings of 'That's Alright' and 'Blue Moon of Kentucky', was auctioned by Christie's on behalf of a British collector. It fetched £99,000.

The music was packaged in an insolent sexuality; youth was libido and authority repression. Liberty was wearing blue suede shoes that year. No wonder Middle America was frightened; what his music was doing to their eardrums, his pelvis was doing to their daughters.

CHARLES NICHOLL,
DAILY TELEGRAPH, 1972

Why, I wonder, do we fail to produce home-grown stars who have the magnitude and the staying power of Elvis? Why didn't Marc Bolan, who died in the same year as Elvis, ever have a chance of rivalling him in the public imagination? Elvis's career was as exceptional as his talent. He made a large number of films but, more than this, he became a *myth*. This is the difference between American stars and their British counterparts. Americans can give their stars mythic status, can load them with awe through careful marketing, skilful agents, manipulation of the media, selected merchandise and appearances planned for maximum impact. Think of Madonna. No ordinary rock star, she's more a global phenomenon.

In the USA Elvis-mania shows no signs of diminishing. It is said that the dead Elvis played his part in the election of President Clinton. (There may be some lessons here for the British premier.) Early on in the presidential campaign, the United States postal service asked people to vote on which of two Elvis images they should use for the new 29 cent stamp that was to be issued in January 1993, the King's 58th birthday. In one picture Elvis was a young rocker with full high-school swoon factor, and in the other a mature, Las Vegas-style entertainer. Overwhelmingly and, commentators say, in the same spirit in which they would choose Clinton, they voted for the young, vigorous Elvis.

As rock journalist and author of *Dead Elvis* Greil Marcus pointed out, while the Democrats celebrated Elvis, George Bush invoked the King as an image of failure and deception in a series of badly judged comments: 'Bill Clinton's been spotted in more places than Elvis' and 'Now we know why Bill always compares himself to Elvis. Every time he has to take a position on something he wiggles.' Bush got it wrong. Elvis, 'a hook lodged in a million hearts', is an icon that demands careful handling.

What are the component parts of an American icon? What are the magic ingredients that elude some stars? Do we sympathise with Liz Taylor when she wants to know: 'What *do* I have to do to become like Marilyn Monroe? *Kill* myself?'

1. THE LIFE
The first thing you'll need, Liz, is a bit of a dodgy start in life, a dramatic reversal of fortune followed by a dark period of unpopularity, then a revival and a showbiz death.

One of the most potent reasons for Elvis's success was his poor 'white trash' background. Here was a boy – a surviving twin (Jesse Garon, born shortly before Elvis, was buried in a shoebox in an unmarked grave) – who picked himself up out of the dirt, hung around radio stations and then one day walked into Sam Phillips's Memphis recording studio (pay two bucks, make a record) to sing a song for his mother's birthday. Sam Phillips was looking for a talent: 'If I could find a white man who had the Negro sound and the Negro feel, I could make a billion dollars.' In Presley he found his dream. A blue-collar truck driver who brought black rhythm and blues into contact with white rockabilly and made a revolutionary, sexy music called rock 'n' roll.

It simply isn't easy to get more than a few clichéd comments out of the man. Conversing with the King is not unlike talking to a pleasant but not particularly articulate farm labourer.

DOMINIC KENNEDY,
RADIO TIMES, 1971

Elvis put the older generation into a confusion of attitudes. His appearance on *the Ed Sullivan Show* in the mid-1950s was permissible *only* if he was filmed from the waist up. He could shimmy, twist, rise up on his toes in a groin-propelled leap, keep guitar and legs on the move yet perfectly in harmony with the voice and the tantalising sudden pauses in the music. He was dangerous, a bit tacky – like the good-looking boys that collect the money on fairground dodgems. By 1957, at the age of 22, he was the most famous man in America.

In the litany of stardom, what followed was inevitable. First a plunge into naff, millionaire's spending – on Graceland, twenty-three rooms of zebra skin, quilted ceilings and gold pianos; on fleets of cars and wardrobes of flashy clothes. He'd buy ten Mercedes at Christmas to give to friends; he

The doo-wop shop.
Central London recording
studios don't have to be
dark-roomed techno
affairs.

bought guns and jewellery and once, famously, a whole funfair so that he could go there unmolested. Michael Jackson couldn't have happened without Elvis, the first template for the pop superstar lifestyle. But, like a football pools winner, the spending is edged with insecurity – what has been called 'the illusion of wealth and the psyche of poverty; the illusion of success and the pinch of ridicule'. Elvis was the poor little rocker, tryin' and spendin' and doin' a Rockefeller. We *felt* for him.

All pure products of America go crazy.

WILLIAM CARLOS WILLIAMS

Elvis's demise and death secured his icon status. The lapse into the gross and barbarously vulgar final stages of his career made him human. He was Fallen, a Sinner and no one (least of all the British) can resist that. By blowing up into a hammy singer in rhinestone flares doing the concert/casino circuit (and being obliged to meet the million-dollar, high-rolling gamblers afterwards) he became a haunting symbol of what America does to its beautiful young talents. He let us watch while his sensual energy ebbed away and was replaced by a bland, fat guy in mother-of-pearl performing for swine.

> You know what's interesting about Elvis? When he was getting ready
> to die, Elvis was broke, wearing big platforms and was like a joke
> in showbusiness. It shows you how fucked up society is, 'cos in the
> movies they only want happy endings and shit. What happened is, when
> this man died, that was their happy ending. Elvis was their American
> dream, the poor boy that got rich and they hated him for it. And
> then he died and they turned him into this god form. And I think
> that's fascinating.
>
> Eddie Murphy, 1990; quoted in *Dead Elvis* by Greil Marcus

2. THE DEATH

Icons don't go quietly. Icons are not left to rest. And wouldn't you believe it, there's talk of exhuming Elvis's body. Questions are still being asked. In the latest twist the report written after the autopsy on Elvis is being re-examined. Murkier questions remain. Was Elvis at the centre of an FBI bonds fraud investigation? Was Elvis killed by the Mafia, anxious that Presley was about to finger some of their head honchos for drug-dealing? Did a hit-man sneak past Presley's sleeping girlfriend and his stoned bodyguard that night and deal a deathly blow, right there in the bathroom? Or did Presley commit suicide, knowing, as one source suggested, that he had bone cancer, or because he was tortured by guilt at having seduced his step-brother's wife? Are we to believe the woman who wrote *Is Elvis Alive?* based on a telephone conversation she had with the star … *in 1988*? Oh yes, if we've learned anything from the USA (Kennedy, Monroe, Lennon), it is that Famous Deaths Cannot Be Simple.

3. THE RESURRECTION

After death, comes industry. Elvis the soap, Elvis the memorial plate, Love Me Tender shampoo. *See* Elvis's toenail, a wart, a lock of his hair in a perspex case. *Buy* a phial of Elvis's sweat, a thimbleful of Graceland dirt, a singing T-shirt. Elvis the reliquary. Elvis the brand name.

Elvis the book title. Albert Goldman made money with his 1981 demolition-job biography of Elvis. The book was low on musical appreciation and high on venom. Goldman, whose book was read widely in Britain, was obsessed with the fat, fading Elvis, dismissing the early years in favour of this:

> The master bedroom – black suede walls, crimson carpets and curtains,
> 81 square feet of bed with mortuary headboard and speckled armrests.
> On the bed lies Elvis himself, propped up like a big fat woman
> recovering from some operation on her reproductive organs.

Curiously, the book left Elvis's dignity undented and smart reviewers considered that the biography gave a clearer insight into Goldman's ambition than it did into Presley's life.

4. THE INTERPRETATION

Dead stars are kept alive in the public imagination through reinterpretation, a fresh account of the life and the talent that can attract a new following. (The Elvis Record and Tape shop in London is full of 17-year-olds.) Elvis was such a contradiction that each generation may make what they will of him. Poor boy or Hollywood star (thirty-three films, mostly mediocre)? Polite-speaking gospel singer or ravaged rocker? Victim of excess or its perpetrator? Someone who *knew* he was a cultural revolutionary or an innocent abroad? A singer of the people or an agent of mass culture? Passive hero or basket case? High art or low rent? You can have the Elvis who said that his favourite singers were Kay Starr and Dean Martin or the one who drank his face off, was a walking drugstore and screwed a lot of young women.

What America is currently making of Elvis (aside from postage stamps) is a nostalgic flag to wave in the face of present uncertainty. Elvis was part of

(Main pic) Bus Stop: Marilyn Monroe 'lookey likey' Pauline Bailey turns heads and the clock back on the King's Road.

(Inset) The well-heeled Duke: Rawhide Shoemakers of Camden Town made most of John Wayne's famous cowboy boots.

America's mythically more splendid past. The 1950s were for Americans what the nineteenth century was for Britain – a period of power and brilliance and growth to be remembered in the long dark nights of an economic downturn. On such nights it is good to watch again the old movie with Dean and Monroe, Coca-Cola and the Hoover Dam, Kennedy, the open range, baseball greats and Presley in his prime. That was the moment of synthesis in America when its violent history of slavery, civil war and gangsterism gave way to calmer prosperity. When racial segregation was outlawed, life was simpler, neighbourhoods still existed and America's energy, like Presley's – raw, young and impetuous – hadn't gone sour.

> Rock 'n' roll is part of a pest to undermine the morals of the youth of our nation. It is sexualistic, unmoralistic and … brings people of both races together.
>
> THE NORTH ALABAMA WHITE CITIZENS COUNCIL, 1955

5. THE TALENT

Elvis may still be a vivid feature of popular culture in Britain because of his role as icon for the United States empire in decline. Certainly he's still instantly distinguishable graphically – the sketchiest outline, the hair and collar, the splayed legs will do – in whatever magazine or on whatever poster he appears, but the life, the death and the Elvis industry wouldn't have been important without his talent, his genius. He was, quite simply, the most affecting of all rock singers. However many imitators there are (and I recommend Paul Chan, an impersonator and fan from Hong Kong who serenades his customers in a white jump-suit at his restaurant, the Gracelands Palace, on the Old Kent Road in London), it's impossible to reproduce the Elvis magic when you first hear:

> She walks like an angel,
> She talks like an angel,
> But I got wise … she's the Devil in disguise.
> From (*You're the*) *Devil in Disguise*, 1963

McDonald's: not so much a burger, more a way of life

Here is a newspaper clipping which, if read by a newly arrived Martian, would tell him much about contemporary America:

> The widow of a Vietnam veteran who shot dead 21 people in a Californian McDonald's in 1984 is attempting to sue the firm, claiming that additives in the burgers caused his 'violent outburst'.

Aside from what it reveals about litigation fantasy (a common complaint in the US) and the national passions for doing things on a big scale, talking in euphemism and buying pump-action weaponry, the story, significantly, names the fast-food restaurant concerned. Because the setting and the accused is no less than McDonald's, the chain which, alongside Coca Cola, is synonymous with the American way of life.

If a person, even one with a Vietnam veteran's pedigree, can have a 'violent outburst' in McDonald's it is more than the murder of those customers that is at stake – it is the idea of family America, and its appointment with Ronald McDonald for a Big Mac or a box of McNuggets before the ball game on a weekend.

America …
an economic system
prouder of the
distribution of its
products than of the
products themselves.
MURRAY KEMPTON,
NEW YORK TIMES

McDonald's opened its first UK restaurant in Woolwich in south-east London in 1974. Now there are 475 branches, 106 of them the drive-through type. Here in Britain too the corporation's red and yellow restaurants typify the American way and stand for much more than the

Food on the move: the
all-American drive-thru
invades the south coast.

finger food which is rushed into the waiting hands of a million customers a day. There are clearly plenty of people who have seen the adverts and want the burgers, but, whether the big Macs at head office in Chicago like it or not, McDonald's also represents the kind of American influence in Britain that is not completely welcome.

What happened in Hampstead, North London, is a good example of this. For twelve years Hampstead kept McDonald's at bay. Local opposition (known as the 'burger-off campaign') was unflagging, the council was sympathetic to the protesters as was Michael Heseltine, who ruled against the fast-food outlet in his first incarnation as Environment Secretary. But in June 1993, the battle was lost and the Big Breakfasts started to roll.

In many of the tabloid press reports local protesters were assumed to be motivated by snobbery, Nimby-ism or queasiness about meat-eating. Certainly, the people they like to call Champagne Socialists may think that McDonald's is to food what Kylie Minogue is to music. But that's not the point. What people were resisting, in one of London's last real villages, was *homogenisation*, turning Hampstead High Street into a clone of every other high street in Britain where, sure as eggs is eggs, McDonald's is quickly followed by Burger King or Wendy or Pizza Hut or Kentucky Fried Chicken or Dunkin' Donut. It's true that in some architecturally sensitive areas McDonald's has been prevailed upon to adapt their standard signage and shop front to respect the look of the street. But these are the exceptions rather than the rule. In many towns in Britain homogenisation is the name of the game. And homogenisation means that eventually we quite literally do not know *where* we are.

The battle has been fought elsewhere. Even in Michigan in the United States, the people of the resort village of Saugatuck gave Big Mac the local equivalent of two fingers when the company attempted to take over a treasured old café called Ida Reds. On a bigger stage the Romans protested because they considered the site at the foot of the Spanish steps less than ideal for a fast food restaurant. It is still there, but living with continued disapproval and the accusation that it 'degrades the streets'.

McDonald's supporters are fond of describing fast food as democratic. To underline the point *everyone* who works for the corporation, from the chairman down, spends time working in one of the restaurants. It is true that McDonald's food is easily understood, easily ordered and easily eaten. Since many Americans like to eat very informally (remember the title sequence of *Roseanne*, where the family meal is a hand-to-mouth dip into an open pizza box?) the food is designed to be eaten not with a knife and fork but with the hands – or one hand if it's a drive 'n' dine customer.

McDonald's has carefully developed an informal, good-fun-for-not-much-money appeal. Its work with sick children, the environmental initiatives and community partnership add to this positive image of McDonaldisation. But that shouldn't prevent us from looking deeper and noticing that McDonald's is also about control, predictability and about reducing food, one of the levelling pleasures of life, to the condition of a factory assembly line product.

What is more, for our British sensibilities, the corporate philosophies of McDonald's are, er, a bit difficult to swallow. Nowhere is this more evident than a few miles away from Hampstead at the Hamburger University in East Finchley.

In a building that looks like a private hospital McDonald's trainees are tutored in the way of the corporation. I joined a session in which a video message from Mike Quinlan, the American chairman and chief executive officer of McDonald's, was being played to a class of young assistant managers. Mike's handsome, ageless face was dark with concern. All was not well in the McDonald's magic kingdom. Despite yearly earnings of $958.6 million, Mike says that customer care has taken a dip, the 'good relationship with turned-on and happy customers' is showing signs of strain: 'You know what's happening? A lot of our customers are getting *divorced* from us. And then what? They're getting *remarried* to the competition. They're *falling in love* with somebody else.'

Mike looks close to tears: 'McDonald's is a wonderful company. I've worked here all my adult life. I hope I *die* here. But this isn't good enough ...'

Wide-eyed, the under-managers – mostly male and wearing white, short-sleeved shirts and grey trousers – sit, like a group of McEvangelists, taking in the word according to Mike. A tutor (wearing a McDonald's signet ring) has given each of them a small, laminated card outlining the corporation's Tips on Approaching and Talking to Customers.

- Use 'props' (coffee refills, mini-cones, etc.)
- Be natural and comfortable.
- Friendly smile. Good eye contact.
- Have some casual conversation to get the ball rolling.
- Introduce yourself. Ask for the customer's name. (Remember it and use it!)

Mac and Bud move at
280mph at Drag Raceway,
Santa Pod.

- Start small. Only one or two minutes.
- Be aware of the customer's 'space'. Don't make them uncomfortable.
- Read the customer. If they seem to be in a hurry, keep it short.
- If the customer is willing to talk, ask some good open-ended questions. (See sample questions on back of card.)

Sample questions, which employees are advised to memorise and not to *read* to customers, include such stunners as: 'Sir, what could we do to improve our service?' and 'Why did you stop at this McDonald's?' The little card wants McDonald's crew members, as the staff are known, to treat customers like friends or valued guests and they are instructed to *know* the customer as they would know their own family – to whom, of course, we often address questions such as 'What could we do to improve our service?' and 'Why did you stop at this house today?'

While few people who have been on the receiving end of British service at its most slouchingly unconcerned will take issue with the principle of giving customer satisfaction, the use of friendship, first names and family ties as the currency of good service only debases both parties. Should a *recorded* voice tell me that 'the company values my call'? (Suppose a person rings up to unleash a string of obscenities?) Should a stranger tell us that he 'remembers the folks we were with last time' or that he's 'been thinking

Kiss goodbye to egg
and chips: Mac and Coke
shine out over Piccadilly
Circus.

about us' when he clearly doesn't know us from a box of eels? In the
United States these routine exchanges mostly pass without notice. But here
it sounds phoney and, in the end, it makes us either peel back our lips and
unwillingly return the false smile or answer with a 'violent outburst'.

The author of the McDonald's phenomenon was Ray Kroc, a milk-shake
mixer salesman who met the McDonald brothers, Dick and Mac, in
California in the early 1950s. They were doing very well out of the
hamburger (and milk-shake) business. Kroc was obsessed with efficiency.
He hated the 'waste, the temperamental cooks, the sloppy service and
food' dished up in the traditional American blue-collar diners and cafes.
He didn't think the hard-nosed, gum-chewing waitresses or insolent truck
drivers were suitable company for families out to eat. What the McDonald
brothers showed him in their short-menu, high-volume restaurant was a
beam of pure light:

> I was fascinated by the simplicity and effectiveness of the system ...
> each step in producing the limited menu was stripped down to its
> essence and accomplished with minimum effort. They sold hamburgers and
> cheeseburgers only. The burgers were ... *all fried the same way.*

Kroc developed this assembly-line idea. (The assembly line had come full circle – car manufacturers had taken the idea from beef-producing abattoirs.) At first he worked in partnership with the McDonalds and then, having built an empire of franchises – an idea pioneered by the Singer Sewing Machine Company – he bought the brothers out for $2.7 million in 1961. By the time of Kroc's death in 1984 the chain was grossing $8 billion a year. McDonald's became a place for 'folks, food and fun', run with a carnival atmosphere for the customers and a set of unbreakable rules for the staff: there were thirty-two slices to every pound of cheese, French fries were cut at 9/32nds of an inch thick … even now machines at McDonald's measure to the second how long a burger or fries are cooked. East Finchley students are told in minute detail how to handle every item they touch – down to the wax paper that's just slippery enough to let the patty glide on to the griddle.

Replicated color and symbol, mile after mile, city after city, act as a promise of predictability and stability between McDonald's and its millions of customers, year after year, meal after meal.

USA TODAY

For a man like Kroc who once had all his managers cut their nose hair for the sake of hygiene, the idea of a restaurant where there wasn't actually any messy, uncontrolled *cooking* seemed ideal. Every franchise was carefully controlled. Usually an individual was allowed only one franchise so that the essential McDonald's way wouldn't be subverted. Staff and franchise trainees were put through repetitive and rigorous training – submitting, if necessary, to nose-hair type indignities.

So, we may not like McDonald's style. Many British people find their insistence on happiness as distasteful as the restaurants' gaudy colours and their evident success. (Just a fraction of the arched M of McDonald's, yellow on red, on a poster is now enough to tell you that fast food is not far away.)

McDonaldisation is a force at work in society which has been identified and examined with great perception and humour by George Ritzer in his book on the subject, *The McDonaldization of Society*. The American fast-food principle, exemplified by McDonald's, is creeping into other, non-edible, sections of our lives.

Is the element of predictability, for example, held up by McDonald's as a virtue (wherever you go, from Beijing to Basingstoke, the product, the setting, is the same), really a virtue at all? Is it in our interests that other corporations now boast this same unerring 'standard', so that 'There are no surprises in a Holiday Inn' became a positive advertising slogan? Taking the principle further still, when Conrad Hilton opened a hotel in Istanbul he proudly declared that 'Each of our hotels ... is a "little America".' Here's the end of geography, the end of travel, the end of the seasons. The corporate aim is to freeze the perfect room, burger, McNugget, hire car, fizzy drink or TV show ready for dumping anywhere in the world – just as though the customer was in Numbskull, Arizona.

And predictability is addictive. Many Americans seem to become disorientated, panicky, even dysfunctional without the reassurance of burger-proximity and guaranteed air-conditioning. Anyone who has ever been a tour guide knows the difficulty of conducting an American group in those regions where 'standards' of food/air/credit card acceptability, etc., are lower than in the United States. In Britain we're developing some of those traits. Some of *us* don't want there to be too many surprises in life either. Why else would (British) people buy (American) camper vans (Winnebegos) in which the mobile world of the van is hermetically sealed to exclude any outside influence – where larder, bed, heating and, most important, toilet are all *known quantities*?

Another consequence of McDonaldisation is the growing emphasis on the quantity rather than quality of what is produced. McDonald's doesn't announce its burgers as 'delicious' or 'spicy'. It describes them as Big or Quarter-pounders. Other companies run with Whoppers, Big Gulps and Big 'uns. Wendy burgers, hoping to catch the market, didn't go out on a limb and make 'mouthwatering' hamburgers – they just made square ones. In the United States restaurants advertise 'The 30-Prawn Dinner', 'As Much Meat As You Can Handle', endless coffee ... it may be bland, it may be disgusting, but at least there's plenty of it.

Blandness in plenty is available in readable form, as subscribers to *USA Today* will be aware. Here is a 'newspaper' which has reduced the events of a complicated world to little snippets of bite-sized news McNuggets. These news gobbets are made more digestible by the addition of pages and pages of celebrity chat, Today's Hero, colour weather charts, sport, Today's Tip Off ... 'Being Tubby is a Good Thing', USA Snapshot and at least one story about the Kennedy family. British newspapers need no tutelage in this kind of journalism, but it is worrying to see them following the American lead in becoming ever more parochial and less willing to challenge the reader with ... the unpredictable.

McDonald's is ubiquitous. This is another source of resentment – even in

American breakfast in an
RV (recreational vehicle):
no nasty surprises in this
home from home.

Britain, where many have made the red and the yellow a part of their way of life. McDonald's has a global grip via its network of franchise holders. Each one, however remote, has been schooled in the American service and profit philosophy, given uniforms (without pockets) for their staff and sent off with a more glowing loyalty to Uncle Sam than the CIA could ever have produced. The price of a Big Mac has become a measure of worldwide inflation: since 1986, *The Economist* has been comparing international costs of living with a Big Mac index.

In the United States there are now 9,300 McDonald's. Half the country's population lives within a three-minute drive of one of the restaurants. So many people have done their (average) four months working in McDonald's that by the turn of the century 50 per cent of the customers will be former employees. Where is the point of saturation? Everywhere in the world people want to eat McDonald's hamburgers. Will McDonald's know when we've all had enough?

Back in East Finchley the class is coming to an end. Having established the meaning of 'pro-active', the students are discussing the companies they remember as having given good service. 'Disney,' says someone on the second row. 'Yes, indeed,' says the tutor appreciatively.

> They pay incredible attention to detail. Do you know that when you park your car at Disney there's someone there to remind you to turn off the lights? And when you get back to the car there's a mechanic who'll come and charge your battery in case you forgot. Now why do they do that …? Exactly. Because they want your last memory of Disney to be a FUN memory. And that's what we're about at McDonald's too.

McDonald's, the edible part of the American entertainment industry, smiles with a smile very similar to that worn by McDisney … but that's another story.

American chrome: fins

Wanna buy a car? Nice runner, immaculate condition, only 384,000 miles on the clock. A snip at £22,000.

Where is the person who is going to hand over 22,000 smackers to a secondhand car dealer in Battersea for a motor that is 35 years old? No sweat. There are plenty of them because this particular dealership, called Dream Cars, doesn't sell glamour-free Hillman Imps, Vauxhall Chevettes and Austin A40s – it sells American classic cars from the post-war period. The £22,000 car in question is a fabulous red 1958 Oldsmobile Rocket 88 with red and white leather interior. It's a rag top and, measuring 19 feet from bumper to bumper, should carry a 'long vehicle' sticker.

When Ralph Nader tells me he wants my car to be cheap, ugly and slow, he's imposing a way of life on me that I'm going to resist to the bitter end.

TIMOTHY LEARY (ATTRIBUTED)

Dream Cars started as a hobby for Milton and Stewart Homan, who soon realised the powerful interest there was in American classic motors in Britain. Theirs is one of scores of garages where enthusiasts go and look longingly at some of the most glamorous motor cars ever built. The Homans travel to America once every three months trawling for cars. Mostly they trawl the west coast – in the California climate cars stand the best chance of avoiding rust.

Steve Berry, who writes for *Classic American* magazine, has his own, well-researched view on why people want to own a 1950s hotrod:

> The people who own these cars are exhibitionists. They want some of that Hollywood sparkle to rub off. And a lot of people are prepared to live on bread and jam in order to own one. You'll find them parked outside the tiniest council house. Some people get into the idea of buying while they're in America on holiday. Since American classic cars rarely cost more than £50,000 (for the most superb, rebuilt model) they're less expensive than British classics.

Bumper to bumper: there's
something blatantly sexy
about classic American cars.

And what is the ultimate, the numero uno car that everyone of these enthusiasts wants to own?

> The 1959 Cadillac is the ultimate icon. It's the biggest, the fastest,
> noisiest, longest, best looking and the sexiest car. It's Jayne Mansfield
> and no mistake.

Directly and indirectly the American classic post-war car owes a great deal to Hollywood. The cinema, especially the newsreels of the period, changed people's perception of time. Events across the world were flashed up on the screen and stories told in a matter of moments. The 1940s and 1950s saw the twentieth-century obsession with speed reach new heights. Men with crinkly hair regularly took off across American salt flats or skimmed British lakes in super-streamlined vehicles in an attempt to break one record or another. Some lost their lives chasing the tail of that extra second.

Speed was exhilarating – it was almost literally to do with leaving the limitations of the old world behind and storming into that bright new future. The perfect expression of this idea was the streamlined car, the car that shook off the solid, tank-like lines of the running-board days and got down long and low on the road (the 1959 Buick Electra stood only 54 inches in height). These new cars were fronted with pointy chrome and backed up with a pair of fins that soared over brake-lamps and exhaust pipes shaped like rocket launchers.

In 1953 Chrysler produced a slim, short compact car. It was a complete flop. What Americans wanted was exuberance and plenty of chrome – 'brightwork' or 'borax', as it was known in the trade, was functionless but could add heavily to the cost of the car. No matter, symbolism was more important than reason. And by 1956, as Peter Lewis remarked in his book The Fifties:

> The front of the Cadillac looked like a chrome version of an
> Oriental shrine, which is what it was: the object of ritualised
> washing and polishing on Sunday morning, an observance
> as solemn as churchgoing, a service of Holy Carmunion.

There were many kings of chrome. George F. Walker (whose salary back in the 1950s was $200,000) was known as the Benvenuto Cellini of chrome. But the real talent was Harley Earl. Earl lived in Hollywood where his family's firm made, significantly, customised cars for film stars. He acknowledged Cecil B. de Mille as one of his most powerful influences. He joined General Motors in 1928 and his impact was enormous. He styled cars (using clay models to sculpt the initial design) that were different every year. He turned cars and the desire for the latest model into one of the commands of fashion. During his reign new models came out at an astonishing rate – up to nineteen a year – each one an essential topic of neighbourhood conversation.

Under his influence cars sprouted fins, shone with brightwork and wore two-tone livery. Earl was inspired by air and space travel. Just before Pearl Harbor, at an airfield near Detroit, he happened to see an early production model of the Lockheed P38, a revolutionary fighter plane designed by Clarence Johnson. It had elegant streamlined engine mounts and twin tail-booms. It was a revelation. And in 1948 the Cadillac became the first car to pay tribute to aerodynamics with a pair of discreet fins. (Ironically in Britain the fins and aerodynamic styling turned up in some strange places – vacuum cleaners, carpet sweepers, radios and jukeboxes had bits of chrome added to them which were intended to convey that thoroughly modern technology was at work.)

I was in another big cab, all set to go hundreds of miles across the night, and I was happy! The new truck driver was as crazy as the other one and yelled just as much. Now I could see Denver looming ahead like the Promised Land, way out there beneath the stars, across the prairie of Iowa and the plains of Nebraska, I could see the greater vision of San Francisco beyond, like jewels in the night.

JACK KEROUAC, ON THE ROAD

The fins grew and grew and Harley Earl's flight of fancy reached a peak in 1959 with the production of the Cadillac Eldorado. Its tail-fins flared up to an astonishing height, each bisected by a pair of streamlined tail-lights. In the words of Owen Edwards, author of *Cadillac*:

> The vast grille and wide bumpers with protruding rubber-tipped points gave a feeling that the car could devour blacktop, an entire lane at a time. It was as if, with the 1959 model, Harley Earl and his merry band of stylists had decided to weed out those habitual Cadillac buyers who were insufficiently devoted to the breed and build something that demanded deep convictions and courage.

Having had the courage to buy the Caddy (and going into debt for General Motors was widely regarded as a patriotic deed), you needed the spirit to complete the dream implicit in ownership – the spirit to get on the open road. And here the story comes full circle to Hollywood. Modern American cinema has made 'the road movie' a genre of its own.

'Wherever we're going, man, I'm ready!' yells Jeff Bridges as he jumps into Clint Eastwood's Oldsmobile in *Thunderbolt and Lightfoot* (Michael

(Right) Oversized and over here, but don't you just love'em?

(Below) These cars ain't made for parking, they're for cruising.

(Above) Clean mean
machine: for many, the
Harley fulfils the need to
polish all things beautiful.

(Left) Easy riders take
it easy.

Cimino, 1974). This is the total statement of road movie philosophy – young, independent, impetuous and keen to unleash the thunder from a huge V-8, edge the shift-lever through 'R' and 'N' to 'D', boot the gas and take off in a squeal of glory across America …

Just you and your Caddy or Chevvy (or Harley Davidson) finding out what it is to be in America, if things go better with Coke, whether cops are wimps, if morality is intact and other Great Road Questions.

John Ford's classic movie adaptation of Steinbeck's novel *The Grapes of Wrath* was one of the first films to put a hero (albeit an escaped convict buckling under the weight of 1930s' poverty) behind the wheel on Route 66, America's highway of the dispossessed. Ford used the journey to give a panoramic view of contemporary America, in all its bleak grandeur and human misery. Henry Fonda's character, of course, predates the affluent days of autos with fins, but the movie puts the car at the centre of an American epic where it effectively replaces the wagons and horses of the previous generation. Ford also explores the national *restlessness*, the American desire to keep moving.

A little Death each Day … A lot of Love each Night! They treated beautiful women as though they were fast cars … ROUGH.

POSTER FOR
THE YOUNG RACERS, 1963

The immense landscapes associated with the best American road movies (*Vanishing Point, Two Lane Blacktop, Last American Hero, Easy Rider, Electra Glide in Blue, Wild at Heart, Thelma and Louise*) make them difficult to re-locate in a European context. The approach to Bristol, going west on the M4, rarely puts one in mind of the Promised Land. But the outlaw on the run, the male drifter escaping narrow-hearted consumerism and narrow-minded parents in search of a lost frontier, the hero driver in whose car or truck freedom is realised and honour upheld – these ideas are universal and, doubtless, they are there in the locker-room of the imagination when a man spends £22,000 on a dream car.

Slick-tech city

From the Fatboys Diner on Bishopsgate you can look straight across to the largest slab of redevelopment seen in the City of London since the Great Fire of 1666. Over the top of your grits and root beer what you can see is the eastern face of Broadgate, a city within a city – a British version of the Rockefeller Centre complete with pubs, shopping arcades, restaurants, piazzas, prestigious sculpture and an ice rink (Torvill and Dean have glided across it approvingly). And, of course, massive amounts of office accommodation, dealt out in parcels of half a million square feet, the equivalent of five horizontal Empire State Buildings.

The lion's share of this and many other developments in the City and Docklands has been the work of American architects. Americans, in fact, have been at both ends of the revolution that has taken place in the capital since the late 1970s.

It's not the first time the Americans have ridden into London on a wave of commercial enthusiasm, their building plans tucked under their arms. One of the first arrivals was Gordon Selfridge in 1906. Selfridge had been a manager of the Chicago department store Marshall Fields and he brought to London not only something of that new mass-consumer culture, but a bit of American glamour (heavily underpinned by Hollywood). He also brought with him the ideas of Daniel H. Burnham, the architect who built the Chicago store and gave it the confident air of a Renaissance palace. London's Selfridges was built with the same generosity of scale, panache and, incidentally, the same elaborate clock as part of the sumptuous detailing.

During the inter-war years Americans and American wealth came to London in plenty. And it wasn't just retailing that brought them.

For tall or tallish buildings, the Americans have evolved a sort of neo-Roman style that has become to them an accepted symbol of high finance. It is a style of architecture in which pictorial value dominates.

ANDREW RABENEK,
ARCHITECTS' JOURNAL, 1990

Downtown Boston?
There are some subtle
giveaways in Docklands.

International competition in trade and the breakdown of tariff barriers drove American companies to Britain and specifically to London where, by the 1930s, the population had reached eight million. Many of the great household brand names of those days – Gillette, McLeans, Remington, Firestone, Ford and Hoover – were produced in splendid purpose-built factories to the east and west of London. They were the temples to the new gods of consumer durables – drugs, gramophones, toiletries, cosmetics, car accessories and vacuum cleaners that *looked* like car accessories – the thesis was that the factory was no longer simply about production but about marketing and selling as well.

The Hoover factory (still standing but now a Tesco superstore) built between 1932 and 1935 was a *tour de force*. The Wallis–Gilbert partnership's aim was to build factories that dignified the workplace and expressed the commercial pride of the clients. And the factories were built fast. The company used bonus clauses to encourage subcontractors to greater speed. Thomas Wallis's speech to the Royal Institute of British Architects in 1933 incorporates much of the thinking behind *today's* 'factories' of finance:

> The industrial architect should endeavour to give a pleasing effect to his facades … money wisely spent in the incorporation of some form of decoration, especially colour, is not money wasted … good workers look upon their business buildings with pride … and anything that focuses the attention of the public is good advertisement.

At the same time as factories were being built along the Great West Road, new industries were developing in the centre of town. The J. Walter Thompson advertising agency was one of the early tenants in Bush House, at the end of Kingsway, built by the American Irving T. Bush as a trade centre in 1935.

Americans living in London, especially those living it up (hoping to hear nightingales in Berkeley Square), made a significant impact on the West End. Out went the old order of aristocratic mansions on Park Lane – Dorchester House and Grosvenor House were demolished to be replaced by hotels and serviced apartments in a blatantly New York style. In ten years Americans managed to blur the distinction between Park Lane and Park Avenue.

The second wave of American building, the fast-track construction of the 1980s, was concentrated in the City of London. Broadgate, a set of impressive groundscrapers, was the first conspicuous symbol of the Big

Bang and the twenty-four-hour trading world. The development emphasised that London's future lay in being at the crossroads of international finance between New York and Tokyo. Encouraged by the American example, the City had to roll up its striped shirtsleeves, make deregulation happen and stake a claim as the global capitalist casino.

The success of that enterprise, in the early and mid 1980s at least, brought American financiers and business people to London. Once here, they further influenced the life of the city by insisting on buildings that could accommodate the new scale of trading and which expressed their company aspirations or corporate creed. Buildings, in other words, of the sort found in Chicago, Dallas and Lower Manhattan.

> American conglomerates moving into London have little interest in rabbit warren Victorian blocks or older glass towers but rather, want layers of dealing floors buried in wide efficient structures. Hence, the move of Salomon Brothers to 200,000 square feet over Victoria Station and the interest of Morgan Stanley in the new office towers in Canary Wharf.
> *Financial Times*, July 1986

The new trade revolution which reached a climax in London in the mid 1980s needed factories, but not of the Art Deco Hoover type. London's nineteenth-century importance as a trade and banking centre (which had been built on imperial expansion) was maintained even when the colonial pink bits on the map had shrunk considerably. In the 1930s there were still over eighty foreign banks in the City and the numbers were rising. During the 1970s the numbers of banks and subsidiaries of major foreign financial institutions which were involved in financing trade and funding long-term capital, doubled until in 1987, just before the October Stock Market crash, there were 453 institutions directly or indirectly represented in the City.

Several factors contributed to this astonishing growth of London as the 'wholesale market' of international finance. In the 1970s OPEC's petrodollars flowed richly through London banks and proved a considerable magnet for financiers (especially American) to make a base in the City. In 1979 exchange controls were abolished; London was freer of regulation than New York so it was cheaper to make international loans from London than elsewhere. The Eurobond business came to be overwhelmingly centred on London.

As business grew, multinational companies were drawn to London and they brought their need for global financial services with them. London

(Overleaf top left) Canary Wharf, as famous for its financial problems as for its appearance.

(bottom left) Old attitudes and new threats still hinder the development of Docklands.

(top right) Identity crisis: without a central living community, Docklands could remain a ghost town well into the next century.

(bottom right) Beauty or the Beast? The Pelli Tower, which dominates the Docklands skyline, is the only European building with a stainless steel skin.

had in place all the support services, such as foreign-exchange brokerage, legal and insurance services, as well as good communications and a world language. The Thatcher government was committed to *laissez-faire* and in October 1986 deregulation, the Big Bang, obliged the Stock Exchange to abandon its fixed commissions on securities dealing and open up its doors to overseas members.

When those doors opened the Americans (very closely followed by the Japanese) came surfing in on the crest of the second London wave. They came in the form of financial conglomerates which combined banking, dealing and currency trading, buying up the expertise of Stock Exchange firms to become the new 'market makers' of 1986. They employed staff on a massive scale. The US firms Merrill Lynch and Shearson Lehman each had 1,400 people working for them, while Goldman Sachs and Salomon Brothers had well over 700 employees largely involved in the kind of noisy dealing that the film *Wall Street* made famous. For this global scale market-making dealers needed electronic hardware and plenty of it.

Imagine it then. The thousand-year-old City of London, for so long a bowler-hatted, mahogany-panelled gentleman's club, where rents were stable and buildings protected by a strong conservation lobby, is suddenly confronted by an army of Michael Douglases screaming for space, screaming for somewhere to plug in a squillion-poundsworth of IBM instant access to trading heaven. What were they to do? Some 75 per cent of all the office stock in the City had been built before the advent of the personal computer. The buildings were small: mostly they could provide up to 50,000 square feet of office space. The multinationals wanted 500,000 square feet – 600 desks in the same room. There were planning regulations … Wild-eyed, the City looked to government. Government shrugged its shoulders.

The City convulsed, aware that in Docklands the Americans and others were planning an outflanking manoeuvre, a new city to threaten the old. There was no option. Planning controls were relaxed and between 1985 and 1991 nearly 50 million square feet of office space was provided in the City, much of it in buildings far larger than London had ever seen before. It is interesting that just as the brash energy of the new (American and American-style) traders cut through time-honoured City tradition, so the (American and American-style) buildings that housed those traders, were feared as an intrusion of brash Chicago taste.

Certainly the buildings had size in common with their American counterparts. They were characterised by a deep floorplan, vertical and horizontal 'cores' for the technology supply and, usually, a central atrium and skylight. This was the classic post-modern solution which allowed the dealers to enjoy their information revolution surrounded by greenery and plenty of light.

But there was something more. American architectural practices such as Skidmore, Owings and Merrill (SOM), Cesar Pelli and Kohn, Pederson, Fox were chosen to build the Big Bang developments because, frankly, they didn't mess about telling the clients what they ought to build, they got on with giving them what they wanted. British architecture, despite a cluster of brilliant stars – Foster, Rogers, Grimshaw and Farrell – had a reputation for producing beautiful buildings on paper, but very few on the ground. What is more, the work of those few stars apart, London had been blighted by a fatal combination of greedy, insensitive institutional commercial clients and architects content to let choppy brickwork, horrible windows and poor attention to public spaces pass as their best work. British architects had, without too much help, turned the country into a nation of modern-building-haters. The Americans could hardly do worse.

SOM, who built most of Broadgate, part of the Canary Wharf complex and, more recently, several buildings in the Ludgate development, are a good example of the businesslike American approach which City developers found so winning. SOM had plenty of experience in Chicago and elsewhere of building big. They pioneered the use of advanced computer techniques to help solve structural problems. In common with other American firms they had seen the effects of deregulation in the United States several years before it happened here and had watched the evolution of schemes such as Pelli's World Financial Center in New York, the role model for Canary Wharf.

With American experience in mind, SOM weren't going to sit around wringing their hands over what the planners *might* allow, what *might* be possible ... They took bold decisions, produced bold designs that matched architectural expression with good sound engineering and then got on with it. And what SOM buildings might have lacked in high concept, or innovation, they made up for in their attention to detail and their glossy finish.

American companies had a refreshing attitude towards construction too: a classless approach which, instead of treating site managers as so many oiks in boots and hard hats, actually made them part of the professional team

(Above) Milton Keynes Central Rail Station looks more like a sub-branch of the United Nations.

(Right) The Liver Buildings on the Mersey were a European attempt to recreate the sea approach into Manhattan harbour.

(Left) The Hoover Building in west London, now a Tesco development behind the deco facade.

(Below) Another view reveals its proximity to traditional suburban England.

and brought them into the construction management system right from the start of the project. Builders and architects worked as a partnership, not as white- and blue-collar adversaries as they so often do in Britain. The result was that the Americans built fast, with fewer mistakes, and they built cheaper. Latterly British firms have cottoned on to this marriage of the art and craft of building which, it has to be said, does work best when the client is interested and well informed (such as Broadgate developer Stuart Lipton).

The Exchange building at Broadgate, its steel outrigging an appropriate salute to the Victorian ironwork of Liverpool Street station below, is an example of the best of what the Americans have built in the City. The fears of the purists about Chicago-brash building being low on social responsibility proved groundless since the whole site is generous in its public space, with its square and cobblestones and plane trees. In the 1960s, the era of such developments as Harry Hyams's Centre Point, there was little regard for aesthetics or urban amenity. Profit and speed were everything. Today profit is still important but, as Lipton puts it, 'good architecture sells and rent-slabs don't'.

The Americans have been a powerful force in commercial building since the 1980s, even when they have not been the hired architects. The vitality and the vulgarity of post-modern buildings constructed in the City in this period are clearly rooted in the USA and owe much to the influence of architects like Michael Graves and Robert Venturi. Post-modern architecture is sometimes dismissed as the architecture of the entrepreneur (or in this country as the architecture of the Thatcher era, with all the moral and political judgements that that implies). Critics lampoon its 'clip-on' façades of imitation masonry and marble, condemning the designs as being all style and no content.

But others welcome its diversity, its mixture of the old and new, the real and ideal, its wit and the break it represents with the flat, functional seriousness of modernist buildings. Many applaud the Americans for being the first to wriggle out of the strait-jacket of modernism, for calling a halt to the kind of control exerted over people by architects such as Mies van der Rohe, who insisted that tenants in the Seagram Building could only have white blinds and that these had to be set at a specified point between open and closed, so as not to spoil the purity of the building from the outside.

With some lapses of taste (SOM's building at 10 Cabot Square in Canary Wharf perhaps) the Americans haven't done badly in the City and they've certainly given the British a run for their money. The very existence of Canary Wharf, a grand scheme completed with scarcely a building hitch in less than four years, seems to mock the feeble efforts of the British property industry, which could manage only a poorly appointed zoo of unrelated buildings in the rest of Docklands. Londoners have become fond of Pelli's monumental tower, though they might just wonder, as the sun flashes against it in the evening, whether the building also represents North American hot-headedness – there's a chance, after all, that before it's even fully let and before it's been made accessible by proper public transport, it will be out of date, a big, stranded, beautiful white whale.

Has there ever been another place on earth where so many people of wealth and power have paid for and put up with so much architecture they detested? I doubt it seriously. Every child goes to school in a building that looks like a duplicating-machine replacement-parts wholesale distribution warehouse.

TOM WOLFE,
FROM BAUHAUS TO OUR HOUSE

WHO NEEDS A RESIDENCE, JUST LIKE THE PRESIDENT'S?

The new architecture and the expanded invisible earnings that flowed into the City on 100,000 screens left many older buildings defunct. What is now called the Bow Quarter, just off the Mile End Road, was a quintessentially nineteenth-century structure – a huge brick-built factory where, for 100 years, Bryant & May made matches (and where, incidentally, the match girls held their famous strike in 1888). There being no industrial use for the building now, its only future was in conversion to residential use. The property was big enough to house several hundred flats.

As with the converted warehouses of Docklands, Loft Living was the concept used to sell the apartments. The Bow Quarter brochure, subtitled 'The Little Apple', underlined the idea by showing a yellow New York cab on the front cover. Inside, against a picture of a cool, blond guy playing a saxophone to his girlfriend (she's in a white bathrobe) in a living space that looks like a Victorian schoolroom with high-tech additions, the copy explains:

> Loft Living began in the 1950s when artists and writers started living and working in defunct factory space in the commercial areas of downtown New York. The radical departure in lifestyle gave them space and light within a raw, industrial environment.

(Right) Slick-tech
materials are used in the
Broadgate development
near Liverpool Street
Station in London

(Below) The big bucks:
Paul Preston
(McDonalds), Penny
Hughes (Coca Cola),
Richard Oster (Cookson)
and Robin Buchanan
(Bain and Co.) meet to
discuss the US business
invasion.

(Above) Business playgrounds: huge white walls provide tanning opportunities.

(Left) Looking to the future - but did the developers have more money than sense?

These faultless credentials of American urban life were reinforced, during the 1980s, by a collection of loft-lifestyle advertisements for designer beers, financial services and television and audio equipment.

The American appeal of the apartments (don't call them flats) is achieved by implying that a fast, high-flyers' way of life is almost inevitable once you move in. There are lots of perforated steel staircases, wire balustrades, power showers that really work. (British shower heads are well known to be merely decorative.) There is a laundry room on each floor where, one day, a young hunk may take off his Levi's and put them into the Ameri-washer, right there in front of you. Singles fun is also implicit in the Bow Quarter's gym, swimming-pool, sauna and steam-room (who needs Gold Blend?) where young executives keen to invest in personal fitness can meet and pump iron before the creative work of the day.

The truth of the Bow Quarter and its clones (Alaska Apartments, Bermondsey; the King's Cross Marina development overlooking the Grand Union Canal; the planned Manhattan lofts in the old Marquee Club in Soho) is that in one major respect they are unlike New York lofts. They are small. There may be a 9 foot window but the basic flat at the Bow Quarter is itself only 9 feet wide! Never mind. The building has the American-inspired security factor – twenty-four-hour porterage and patrols – and will soon have a diner-style restaurant in one of the basements off Times Square. The suspension of disbelief may not be total, but at prices from £53,000, the little Apple comes close enough to being the Real Thing.

Remote control

The cartoonist Heath could easily make the Americanisation of British television a subject for his endlessly chattering Great Bores of Today. An open-mouthed diatribe by a spindly illuminati might go like this:

> … never watch it myself it's all imported stuff Cagney and Lacey are past it I think Baywatch is just beefcake airheads did you see the man on Oprah who slept with his twin brother I prefer reading these days satellite's no better in America some people can get six hundred channels it'll never happen here shame about Cheers though remember the one where a drunk comes in wearing a bathrobe …

We're ambivalent about TV from America. On the one hand there has been enthusiasm for American innovation and verve. (Remember how British television started? It had all the starchy formality of a concert performance, with announcers in dinner jackets and programme intervals during which serious music would be played over pictures of fish or a potter's wheel.) And there has been affection for a lifetime of American shows, from *I Love Lucy* to *Roseanne*. On the other hand, there is a gnawing fear that what we perceive as the worst aspects of US television (what you'd see on your TV in a Howard Johnson motel room) – a kind of bewildering cacophony of channels all racing downmarket after bigger slices of an increasingly fragmented audience – will come here and make *The Jewel in the Crown* and *Prime Suspect* nothing more than relics from a vanished age of broadcasting. With the BBC heading, logically, towards relegation as nothing more than a programme publishing house, and with many commercial companies left dangerously short of programme-making money after the franchise débâcle, we're especially rattled by what we read of the United States television business; by ratings

> *I asked why so many Argentines disliked the United States. The reply came with a rush - Envy!*
>
> JOHN GUNTHER,
> INSIDE SOUTH AMERICA.

The rooftops of London:
how long before someone
invents a mock-Victorian
satellite dish?

wars, channels being whipped by advertisers, the control of television by dangerously few global media corporations. Now, when we say that it could never happen here, there is a quaver in our voice.

In 1983, a Californian called Jack Mingo invented 'couch potatoes' and their wives/girlfriends, 'couch tomatoes'. The success in Britain of his *Official Couch Potato Handbook* (and the phrase itself) revealed another of our deep-seated fears – that, like the Americans of our imagination, we'd turn into flabby, undiscriminating viewers, junked out on games shows and soaps, a cola in one hand, a packet of O'Grady's au gratins in the other. Mingo suggested that potential potatoes could self-diagnose by answering the following questions:

- Are moments spent in front of the Tube some of your fondest childhood memories?
- Do the people on the TV screen seem more real to you than your family and friends?
- Do you ever lie about how much TV you watch?
- Do you ever 'bliss out' in front of TV and forget what you're watching?

Mingo needed no greater proof that the British could grow their own couch potatoes than the story of Charlotte Gardener. Charlotte, a keen television viewer from London, kept her television set switched on night and day for two years. Eventually a component burned out and the fumes killed her.

The knee-jerk expression that is often used to describe (and account for) the numbers of American programmes which are making couch potatoes of us all is 'media imperialism'. It is a phrase which generates more heat than light. Imperialism is a pejorative word in this context and it implies a deliberate attempt to win the hearts and minds of people by infiltrating and manipulating the mass (not the high) culture. The French, much more than the British, have been alarmist about American cultural intentions in Europe, hence this description from *La Guerre Culturelle* by Henri Gobard (1979):

> Conventional warfare struck at the heart to kill and then conquer; economic war struck at the belly to exploit and acquire riches; cultural war strikes at the head to paralyse without killing, to conquer by slow rot, and obtain wealth through the disintegration of cultures and peoples.

But this is to underestimate people, who are not so easily uprooted from their culture. Think of the efforts made by the USSR to control the populations of its satellite states – propaganda was daily pumped out on screen and in print. The state hoped to wield influence by restricting the public media diet to only those items which the regime found palatable. It didn't work. Worse, from the Soviet point of view, it served to redouble the intense interest shared by almost everyone east of Berlin in Western books, television, magazines, black market videos (and the jeans that people in those videos were wearing).

The importation of programmes does not stop people being themselves – or reacting to those programmes through the filter of a national sensibility very different from that of the original (American) audience for whom the programmes were intended. Even in Latin American countries, where the United States is a strong, close presence, the people still have a fierce sense of their Latin and Catholic culture. Despite the fascination with Uncle Sam's credit cards, fast food, white-walled tyres and Virginia tobacco, which might be said to be a by-product of American television, there's a cynicism, even a loathing, of real American intervention, of the political Big Brotherhood. American *cultural* influence, in other words, may be wide, but it isn't very deep.

'Cultural imperialism' is a misbegotten expression. That is not to say that American companies, including world telecommunications networks, aren't expansionist and aren't sometimes helped by the US government. They are. It is not to say that the United States doesn't finance some 'cultural services' abroad, such as the Voice of America radio station, or that American products don't sell better where the population has been softened up by television images. But to portray viewers of American television and films as merely passive recipients of an alternative ideology is too simplistic.

In Britain cries of doom and gloom were raised recently when the consultants Booz, Allen and Hamilton presented a report to the House of Commons National Heritage Committee on Broadcasting. The report predicted that by the year 2000 only 13 per cent of all programmes on our screens, including news, would be British in origin. (At the moment the BBC originates 62 per cent of its programmes, Channel Four 53 per cent. Most of the bought-in programmes are from America.) But, as Brenda Maddox pointed out in the *Daily Telegraph*:

> Percentages are meaningless. Percentage of what? The share of British
> production is going to decrease only because the total number of channels
> is going to increase … more than 100 will be available.

What is more, predictions tend to ignore the obvious truth that what audiences like best is the home-grown product, and that at the moment this doesn't seem likely to be replaced by the thematic offerings of satellite channels or a non-stop menu of Hollywood films.

Looked at more closely, what seems to be a sickly one-way traffic in programming often turns out to be healthy trade. One of the more interesting aspects of Jack Mingo's paperback survey of television is that British programmes occupied several places in the Couch Potato Membership Poll All Time Top 100, which ran:

1	The Twilight Zone
2	M*A*S*H
3	Star Trek
14	The Prisoner
16	Monty Python
21	The Avengers
51	Fawlty Towers
72	Benny Hill

In the future the overabundance of channels in the United States will force the Americans to import more programmes, just as we are doing. Many people would greet this with cries of 'whoopie!', hoping that it might begin to limit some of the isolationism which has led to Americans having an imperfect knowledge of the rest of the world.

In cable and satellite television America has led the way. Cable started in Pennsylvania and Oregon in the early 1950s, bringing local and network programmes to communities where over-the-air reception was blocked by mountainous terrain. For extra cash subscribers watched, in 1962, the heavyweight boxing match between Sonny Liston and Floyd Patterson. Lights came on in entrepreneurial minds, and cable expanded with Home Box Office – a service which started in 1975 with seventy hours of weekly movie programming supplied by United Artists/Columbia Cablevision.

Sport is now the major commercial reason for cable and satellite television in the United States. So closely woven are these two strands of American business that some TV moguls such as Ted Turner have *bought* their own teams (the Atlanta Braves baseball team and the Hawks basketball squad) in order exclusively to broadcast their games across the nation with, of course, a firm hand on the advertising, merchandising and image manipulation needed to generate the teams' popularity.

In the creation of the Premier Division in British football, the introduction of cheerleaders on the touchline and the payment of unprecedented fees to football clubs (BSkyB recently paid £1.5 million to Spurs for rights to show their games, a sum which helped stave off financial collapse), we see emerging in Britain something of the American interdependence between sport and television. We've bought the idea of 'junk sport' too, in the hulking shape of the bouts staged by the World Wrestling Foundation – part circus, part comic book, part reason to shave off that Zapata moustache.

There is American money in satellite television (and much in the slowish business of establishing cable systems in the UK). The non-terrestrial channels *do* take a lot of imported product from the United States, but increasingly in our homogenised society, this appears as just part of a generalised, international type of entertainment. The 1993 *British Film Institute Film and TV Handbook* lists the channels planned for the near future: The Ability Channel (community programmes); BBC-Sky News Channel; China News Europe; The Country Music Channel; European Christian Television; The Games Channel (with interactive element); The Ideas Factory Network (arts and music); ITV Channel (Central/Carlton/Meridian); The Property Channel; and UK Gold (BBC/Thames entertainment – now up and running, with repeats of *British* television favourites).

A good example of an American initiative which now has international, even global, appeal is MTV. Music Television is part of the Viacom Corporation, which belongs, apparently, to the man credited with the invention of the multiplex cinema: 71-year-old Sumner Redstone. MTV reaches 210 million homes around the world. The twenty-four-hour European version of the station, like its American cousin, plays music video clips, together with news, movie information, promotions and tour information, and is strung together by VJs with names like anagrams – Steve Blame, Marijne van der Vlugt, Rebecca de Ruvo, Doctor Dre, Pipp Dann. It feeds off the homogenised world of pop music.

Yet European MTV cannot be dismissed as a bland American spin-off. Technically it has been a shot in the arm for many youth and arts programmes on terrestrial channels in Britain, widening their visual language. The station's highly original idents, its use of graphic stings, innovative title sequences and, following on from the French New Wave, its elliptical editing and juxtaposition of black and white and colour images have become the stock-in-trade of every show that has arty or youthful pretensions. The shoestring budgets on which some music videos are made has led to the rediscovery of hand-held camera work, the reprocessing of footage and inventive manipulation of images on the screen. The more expensively made videos are spiked with every type of footage in quick-fire succession, from archive to animation. The results of this broadening of the visual language are now watched, by viewers who have never even seen MTV, in programmes such as *Panorama*.

Even in the film industry, importing material can be a spur to inventiveness and *needn't* spell the end of the home product. During the 1980s Japan and France were the main importers of US movies – yet these countries also have the liveliest and most prolific domestic film industries.

We are not going to drown in American entertainment. There *are* other dangers from American film and television against which we should be on our guard in Britain. But before sounding those alarms, what about a quick celebration of some of the American talent that has been worth watching since the box first started flickering in the corner of our living-rooms?

In the beginning was the Game Show. The hundreds of blameless early evening half-hours we've all spent watching conveyor belts, flashing lights, turning wheels, mystery boxes, unfinished crosswords and little-known celebrities struggling to complete phrases such as 'A stitch in time is worth … er … doing?' can be attributed to the work of two all-American geniuses, one of whom grew up on a chicken farm, while the other spent his early years as a boxing promoter. Excellent backgrounds in their different ways for Mark Goodson and Chuck Barris respectively, the undisputed kings of the game show.

Goodson, in common with many television talents (and the mighty Orson Welles), started in radio. He produced radio soaps, wrote for variety shows and then, in 1946, he sold his first network game – *Winner Takes All*. His inventions in the years that followed became familiar to British audiences: *What's My Line?* (CBS 1950–67); *The Price is Right* (NBC 1956–63); *Match Game* (NBC 1962–9), which in Britain became the BBC's *Blankety Blank*; *Call My Bluff* (NBC 1965); and *Family Feud* (ABC 1976), which became *Family Fortunes* on ITV.

Contrary to popular belief, big money prizes are an exception to the rule in American game shows, after a national scandal in the 1950s found that the legendary *$64,000 Question* and a show called *Twenty One* had been rigged. In Britain, cash prizes are rigorously monitored by the regulators and banned altogether by Channel Four, and other prizes are modest.

We've borrowed American styling when it comes to game-show hosts – there's the same chatting to guests, boom-boom delivery of well-honed one-liners and the device of awarding a lot of exciting points at the beginning and the end of the game. Careful observers credit American hosts with having better teeth (or caps) and haircuts than their British counterparts but rate them lower on 'sincerity', or the illusion of the same. What we don't (yet) have nearly as much of as US game shows is audience euphoria shading into hysteria shading into mass loss of control of bodily function.

Chuck Barris, the promoter who also distinguished himself by writing a hit tune for Freddie and the Dreamers (what kind of training do you *need* to be a game-show inventor?), took the programme format on from the parlour-game-with-famous-ish-panellists model. He developed *The Dating Game* (ABC 1965–73), which we know as Cilla's *Blind Date*; *The Newlywed Game* (ABC 1966–74), which became *Mr and Mrs*; and *The New Treasure Hunt* (syndicated 1974–7), which, in its British form, made Anneka Rice's bottom very famous indeed.

You can learn more about America watching one half hour of Let's Do A Deal *than by watching Walter Cronkite for a whole month.*

MONTY HALL,
US GAME SHOW HOST.

Barris discovered that much entertainment value was to be had from embarrassing and humiliating 'regular' people in game shows where they would readily exchange a bit of foolishness for 15 minutes of fame. It was what the media historian David Marci in his book *Prime Time, Prime Movers*, called a 'revolt against the antiseptic atmosphere dominating mass culture production values in the late 1970s'. Some of the early prototypes of this expanded game show were excruciatingly embarrassing. I remember seeing a show in which the central activity was throwing money from the window of a high building somewhere in America and then filming bewildered people in the street below as they scrambled to pick it up. Good taste put paid to that show before a 10 ton truck did. Also in receipt of the raspberry was Chuck Barris's show called *How's Your Mother-in-Law?*, in which three celebrities 'rated' the mothers-in-law of three non-celebrity couples. In the show that 'put the legendarily frightening and meddlesome battle-axe in the hot seat' families were expected to supply shocking personal details and horrific stories about these women.

The logical next step after putting Joe Public in front of the camera was to

Beam me up Scotty?
Real couch potatoes can
escape into The Twilight
Zone twenty-four hours
a day on video.

put him behind it too. British programmes along the lines of *You've Been Framed* followed in the footsteps of American television. However, in the United States, vicarious pleasure does not end with watching the face of a man whose swimming-pool has been turned overnight into a crazy golf course or a bride who falls over and shows her suspenders. In America you can view footage of 'real' drama: life-threatening crimes, people being shot, accidents happening ... a sort of *999* hosted by Jeremy Beadle, and without the happy endings. In that this begins dangerously to blur the distinction between slapstick mishaps and actual harm – reducing both to 30 seconds' worth of wobbly hand-held entertainment – it is a development which I hope we resist in Britain.

Every year when it's Chinese New Year in New York, there are fireworks going off at all hours. New York mothers calm their frightened children by telling them it's just gunfire.
DAVID LETTERMAN.

There are other movers and shakers from American television whose work has had a profound effect in Britain. There was the comedienne Lucille Ball, who co-starred with her husband Desi Arnaz in the *I Love Lucy* shows, which two-thirds of the American population watched between 1951 and 1955. Scatterbrained, pre-feminist Lucy was wholesome enough to represent American womanhood.

Not only did the show establish sitcom as the dominant genre for the presentation of comedy on television (with the American open-plan living area as the main arena for the action – a format that has lasted until *Roseanne* and the present day), but Desilu, the company that produced *I Love Lucy*, was one of the first independents to make a telefilm series. Its success encouraged Hollywood to launch itself, against a background of falling box-office takings, into full-scale television production.

Steven Bochco, the television producer, was the man who gave us *Hill Street Blues* (1980–88), the revolutionary cop show. Starting as a screenwriter on *Columbo*, Bochco brought together the wit and psychological insight of that show, the ensemble acting style of British soaps and the crowd-framing abilities of directors such as Robert Altman to make *Hill Street Blues* a terrific success. Every up-market cop show since has paid tribute to the refreshing realism of its technique – the sense the audience has of being in the hubbub of activity, the treatment of the lesser characters, the inclusion of off-centre, seemingly irrelevant action and the abandonment of boring head-and-shoulder shots.

The man who brought those back – and especially the glittering, padded, almost surgically impossible shoulders – was Aaron Spelling, the creator of *Dallas* and *Dynasty*. These blockbusters seemed to suit the British mood in the 1980s but the mood has passed. An interesting distinction between British and American popular drama audiences is that, for us, real life (*Casualty*, *The Bill*, *London's Burning* – we seem to be obsessed with the emergency services) is more powerful than glamorous, aspirational life plots. The history of British television is scattered with the bodies of programmes which have tried to work in the American genre and failed – *Triangle*, *Howard's Way* and, most recently, *Eldorado* have failed to secure the desired audience. Maybe an inability to take ourselves seriously is part of the trouble or perhaps, as television director David Barrie puts it:

> Nobody seems to be able to come up with a credible script and, however
> much leopard skin you drape around her, Kate O'Mara is a soft-boiled siren.

Ironically what we in Britain have to fear about the American media is not its overbearing success but the possible failure of its mainstream. American network television is in deep trouble, with audiences and advertisers turning to cable and satellite channels which are available in huge numbers. Ten years ago the three main television networks, CBS, NBC and ABC, held 83 per cent of the viewing market in the United States. Now they hold 61 per cent. Commentators have suggested that the last programme to be made for the old mass audience was *Cheers* and that what replaces it (and its kind) is a plethora of special interest group programmes, narrowly targeted to attract Hispanics or Yuppies or Jews or Rappers or Evangelical Christians or people who want to be dolphins. Some argue that this is no bad thing. Hasn't American television, after all, perpetuated the male WASP view of the world for long enough? But separatism has its dangers. In his book *Culture of Complaint* Robert Hughes talks about the 'fraying' of American taste and the dangers of accelerating the sub-divisions in society by, among other things, enshrining them in specialist programming:

> America is a collective work of the imagination whose making never ends,
> and once that sense of collectivity and mutual respect is broken the
> possibilities of American-ness begin to unravel.

In Britain, where society is more cohesive, the old television certainties are less under threat, but it is worth keeping a cautious eye on the American experience. Because stripped of its achievement as a mass medium, the voice by which the nation addresses itself, the prospects for television are rather depressing:

> If television talks to a lonely, divided aggregation of small audiences,
> no matter how much choice is offered, it will have died, becoming
> what Edward R. Murrow, the creator of network journalism, feared
> in 1958: 'Wires and lights in a box.'
> Nicholas Fraser, commissioning editor at Channel Four

Network news programmes in America, which were once a beacon of
modern, informal journalism, are now struggling. Some – and we should
be warned – have gone down the road of 'happy talk' between anchor
people, of filtering the news so that it flows gently into the sea of more
trivial entertainment that keeps the programmes afloat. Local news has
been booming and making profits directly in relation to the number of
exploitative stories along the lines of 'Kiddy Porn in the Mid West: our
exclusive report'. But the strand of Americanisation in British television
that should give us most cause for alarm is dangerous for being least
visible. It is to do with the blurring of distinctions between entertainment
and news (infotainment), between reality and reconstruction, a fusion
which Michael Paul Rogin refers to in his book *Ronald Reagan: The Movie*.

> The oppositions that traditionally organised both social life and social
> critique – oppositions between surface and depth, the authentic and the
> inauthentic, the imaginary and the real – seem to have broken down.

In America we saw the blending of politics and play-acting in Reagan's
'make my day' style of presentation. News and the making of it are no
longer distinct – it is significant that Walter Cronkite was asked to run as
president … twice. And now reconstructions help you to experience
history as entertainment; to Be There – at the Gettysburg Address, the
crucifixion of Jesus Christ and the fall of Troy. David Wolper, the
documentary film maker, made a film about the preservation of animal
species which included a graphic and moving scene of a polar bear being
illegally hunted and killed. It turned out that Wolper had 'recreated' the
event for the cameras, using an actor in a polar bear costume. In America,
there is little restraint on the use of reconstruction in news and current
affairs programmes. Recently, NBC was sued by General Motors for
passing off a filmed reconstruction of an exploding truck as a real event
and as proof of GM's negligent design. We no longer know what is real. As
Lili Berko, an American media commentator, explains it:

> The appeal of simulated imagery lies in its promise to improve on the
> original, to offer an image of the world which is larger than life, to create
> a degree of resolution that is beyond human perception – a hyperrealism.

And you know where that leads? That's right, straight to a perception of
the world borrowed from the theme park …

HeritageLand

The Disney Corporation may have decided to build EuroDisney on the Parisian doorstep, rather than on a patch of marsh land in Essex, but as we shall see, it is nevertheless implicated in what follows. The company responsible for 'the most popular man-made attractions on the planet' is no Mickey Mouse when it comes to influencing our whole philosophy of beyond-the-home, themed entertainment.

In his book *Travels in Hyperreality*, Umberto Eco devotes the title essay to a discussion of the American obsession with 'realism', that is to say with the reconstruction or copying of reality, especially for the purpose of entertainment. He notes the American interest in the diorama, in speaking, moving audio-animatronic figures, in 3D movies and in waxworks. Between San Francisco and Los Angeles there are no fewer than seven 'attractions' offering wax versions of Leonardo da Vinci's painting of the Last Supper. These are regularly displayed with a backing of symphonic music and son et lumière effects ... 'the taped voice informs you that you are having the most extraordinary spiritual experience of your life and that you must tell your friends and acquaintances about it.' An experience that is absolutely fake, is being sold as *better* than the real thing.

Could the last American frontier be an amusement park?

NICHOLAS VON HOFFMAN,
AMERICA ON THE RUN.

Eco visits the Fortress of Solitude in Austin, Texas. This is a surreal monument/personal mausoleum built by President Lyndon B. Johnson during his own lifetime. The recorded voice of Mrs L.B.J. conducts visitors round a building which is part museum, part waxwork exhibit, and contains a full scale model of the Oval Office, a perfect reproduction in every detail, down to the door knobs. Once again, since everything *looks* real, the reproduction assumes an 'authenticity' of its own. It's a vivid example of how many Americans have come to deal with foreign times and foreign places: by faking them.

The passion for reproduction is what is behind the Epcot Centre (part of Disney World in Florida), and is a feature of trade fairs such as Expo '92 in Seville. Here, in 'display cabinets' are countries whittled down to the most obvious stereotypes. At Epcot, the World Showcase (eleven countries) claims to have been motivated by sentiments to do with the Brotherhood of Man and the Fellowship of Nations. In the UK area visitors can, the official guide book says, 'stroll within a few hundred yards from an elegant London square to the edge of a canal and a rural scene, via a bustling urban English street framed by buildings that constitute a veritable rhapsody of historic architectural styles'. In fact it's an absurd confusion of red telephone boxes, a pub selling ale, shops selling china and golfing jumpers, performing Pearly Kings and Queens and a half-timbered emporium selling wooden spoons called The Magic of Wales.

But perhaps the inconveniences, the unfamiliarity of going abroad (even for a seven-day spin round the European capitals) are removed by Epcot? Why visit Venice when you can buy all the authentic merchandise *and* see a half scale model of St Mark's Square without going further than Orlando?

> At one end there's the Heritage Grand Hotel - Georgian on steroids, Monticello mated with Ramada Inn and finished in Wendy's Old Fashioned Hamburger gothic. This is attached to a two-hundred-yard stretch of bogus Victorian house fronts, which screen the shopping mall. The house fronts have extruded plastic gingerbread details and are painted in colours unfit for baboon posteriors.
> P.J. O'Rourke on Heritage USA, the Christian amusement park created by TV evangelists Jim and Tammy Bakker. From *Holidays in Hell*.

In Britain we have busily imported from the United States many of these info-tainment techniques. Not so much (as yet) to reproduce and remodel foreign countries (we're still closer, geographically, to Venice than we are to Epcot) but to produce 'heritage parks' that reproduce and remodel the past.

To take one of many examples at random: at Ironbridge, near Telford in Shropshire there is a museum complex which marks a 'World Heritage Site'. It was here, in 1709, that Abraham Darby pioneered the technique of smelting iron ore with coke, an advance that led to the production of the first iron rails, iron wheels, iron bridges and the production of the first high pressure steam locomotive, and which was the basis for the whole Industrial Revolution and the beginning of the modern world.

Part of the 'Ironbridge Experience' is an open-air museum on a 50-acre site called Blist's Hill which aims to take the visitor back 'into a living community at the turn of the century. Along the gas-lit streets of this Victorian town, past railway sidings, yards and pigsties, shops and offices, hear the hiss of steam and clank of machinery...'. There's a 'working' pub, chemist's shop, bakery, printer, candlemaker and blacksmith where 'workers' in period costume ply their 'trade' and sell the merchandise to the visitors. In each of the houses dotted round the village there are more 'people of the time' – the doctor, the squatter woman, the toll keeper – who will talk about their 'lives' in that curious 'thee and thou' language which is supposed to take us back to the olde worlde.

> *Ed Laird from California could not understand why the Queen was absent. 'When we go to Disneyland, Mickey's there.'*
> SUNDAY TIMES ARTICLE ON THE OPENING OF BUCKINGHAM PALACE TO THE PUBLIC.

What impression do we have of a Victorian industrial town from Blist's Hill? Do we glimpse the flames and fury of the iron works, described by one contemporary observer as looking like 'the cauldron of hell'? Do we catch a whiff of poverty, child labour or anything of the struggle and energy and invention that scorched the name of the place into the history books? We do not. We gawp instead at something that reminds us of a Hovis advertisement on the outside and a Laura Ashley catalogue indoors. We buy our 'hand-made' candle or iron door stop and go home thinking we know a little more about our history.

Of course people enjoy this American-style hyperreal reproduction of the past. I suspect the Victorian age was chosen instead of an earlier period for Blist's Hill because there is pleasure to be had in recognising *that* mangle, *those* jars in the chemist, *this* writing slate in the school house. But people are being robbed as they smile. Not robbed of their money in the shop that turns the past into tea towels and the iron bridge itself into a box of mints, but robbed of a history unclouded by manipulative nostalgia. And, not to be too portentous about it, people without a clear head about the past, rarely have a clear vision of the future. Wouldn't it be the greatest irony if the Americans – once British subjects and still in awe of our history and traditions – were to provide the means by which that history might be rewritten?

(Above) Curious connections: American Indians wave to Fort Apache at Nottingham's Great American Adventure theme park.

(Right) Arthur's Gaff: but is an Englishman's home still his castle, or is it a theme park?

(Left) Going loopy: the Dragon's Lair rollercoaster at Camelot Theme Park in Chorley, Lancashire.

(Below) Manchester boosts its US leisure facilities in case some unexpected guests drop by in the year 2000.

Randall's Guide to the American Way (Over Here)

Great Britain, the 51st State. Well, that may be going a bit too far, but really, when I first came to England 20 years ago it was a totally different place. The only take-away, or as we say 'carry-out' food available was Indian, Chinese or fish and chips, people rented their TVs to watch three channels and the pubs served warm beer.

It is now the 1990s, I have lived here for over fifteen years and this place has sure changed. What was I saying about the 51st State? It is all here: Dial-a-Pizza, McDonald's, American casual wear, cars and memorabilia, cold beer in long-necked bottles, Tex Mex food and great hamburgers.

In order to help you get a taste of the American flavour to be found in the UK, we have compiled a pretty comprehensive listing of some great places to check out and find a good time. After all - that's the American Way.

GREAT AMERICAN INVENTIONS

1856 – Levi Strauss was a poor Jewish boy from Bavaria who went to America aged 18 and worked as a pedlar. In 1856 he set up a worker's clothing shop in San Francisco using material imported from France – *serge de Nîmes* – which was shortened to denim and dyed indigo along the way. The trousers he made from this material were strengthened with copper rivets, and had a double line of stitching on the pockets that symbolised the wings of an American eagle. For almost 100 years Levis led an ordinary life … until James Dean wore them with a cocky hat in the film *Giant*.

CLOTHING & FOOTWEAR

AMERICAN CLASSICS
20 Endell Street
London WC2H 9BD
Tel: 071 831 1210

398, 400 & 404 Kings Road
London SW10 0LJ
Tel: 071-352-3248

AMERICAN COLLEGE JACKETS
Anvill Cottage
Market Lane, Walpole St Andrew
Wisbech
Cambs
Tel: 0945 780136

THE BOOT RACK
Wynn Bank Farm
Wereton Road
Audley
Stoke on Trent ST7 8HE
Tel: 0782 723389

THE BOOTSTORE
161 Kings Road
London SW3 5TX
Tel: 071 351 1610

BUDDIES
Baseball/Softball Clothing
232 Northfields Avenue
London W13 9SJ
Tel: 081 566 4510

EAGLE SPORTSWEAR
Unit 3c
Venture Park Estate
Fareham Road
Hants PO13 0BA
Tel: 0329 285841

FLIP
125 Long Acre
London WC2E 9PE
Tel: 071 836 7044

Unit 1
Town Quay
Southampton

FLIP INCORPORATED
27/29 Bold Street
Liverpool L1 4DN
Tel: 051 708 6067

72 Queen Street
Glasgow G1 3DN
Tel: 041 221 2041

59-61 South Bridge
Edinburgh EH1 1LS
Tel: 031 221 2041

254 Union Street
Aberdeen AD1 1TN
Tel: 0224 626758

8/10 Kirkstyle
Overgate Centre
Dundee DD1 1RE
Tel: 0382 29057

FLIP OF HOLLYWOOD
12/14 Cross Street
Newcastle Upon Tyne
NE1 4XE
Tel: 091 261 8248

LILLYWHITES LTD
Piccadilly Circus
London SW1Y 4QF
Tel: 071 930 3181

RANCH HOUSE
WESTERN STORE
58 Halesowen Road
Netherton
West Midlands DY2 9QA
Tel: 0384 234142

RAWHIDE BOOT REPAIRS
26 Camden Road
London NW1 9DP
Tel: 071 485 2957

RAZORS EDGE
83 Hurst Street
Birmingham B5 4TE
Tel: 021 622 6605

ROCKET LTD
225 Camden High Street
London NW1 7BU
Tel: 071 267 3046

ROCKING EMPORIUM
12 Victoria Road
Swindon
Wiltshire SN1 3AJ
Tel: 0793 542545

SPORTING STYLE
80 High Street
Whitton
Middx TW2 7LS
Tel: 081 894 9210

STORM
Unit 402
The Arcadian
70 Hurst Street
Birmingham B5 4TE
Tel: 021 622 6605

UNCLE SAM'S
86 High Street
Evesham
Worcester WR11 4EU
Tel: 0386 40614

54A Park Street
Bristol BS1 5NJ
Tel: 0272 298404

4 Sydney Street
Brighton BN1 4EN
Tel: 0273 695901

THE VINTAGE
CLOTHING COMPANY
Afflecks Palace
Church Street
Manchester M4 1PW
Tel: 061 832 0548

8-12 Slater Street
Liverpool L1 4BW
Tel: 051 707 2562

WILD CLOTHING
4-6 Broad Street
Nottingham NG1 3AL
Tel: 0602 413928

WHISTLE BAIT
21 Belmont Lane
Stanmore
Middlesex HA7 2PL

RESTAURANTS & DINERS

AMERICAN DINER
350 Kings Road
London SW3 5UU
Tel: 071 376 7128

Trocadero
Rupert Street
London W1V 7FS
Tel: 071 734 0162

AMERICAN SEAFOOD
RESTAURANT
34 Surrey Street
Croydon CRO 1RJ
Tel: 081 686 0586

BELL'S DINER
7 St Stephen's Street
Edinburgh EH3
Tel: 031 225 8116

BIG LUKE'S TEXAS RESTAURANT
45 Bath Lane
Newcastle Upon Tyne NE4 5SP
Tel: 091 230 1022

BJ'S DINER
Unit 108, Savoy Centre
Sauchiehall Street
Glasgow G2 3ER
Tel: 041 353 1571

BREAK FOR THE BORDER
Tex Mex Food & Live Music
5 Goslett Yard
Charing Cross Road
London WC2H 0EA
Tel: 071 437 8595

7-8 Argyll Street
Oxford Circus
London W1V 1AD
Tel: 071 734 5776

BURGER KING
Over 200 Restaurants nationwide,
including:-
118 Princes Street
Edinburgh

Terminal 3
Heathrow Airport

Hilton Park Pavillion Services
Staffordshire

46 Regent Street
London

CHAPLINS AMERICAN
RESTAURANT
22 Grange Mount
Birkenhead
Liverpool L43 4XW
Tel: 051 652 6232

CHEERLEADERS
Albion Wharf
Albion Street
Manchester M1 5LN
Tel: 061 237 1380

CHICAGO PIZZA PIE FACTORY
CHICAGO RIB SHACK
CHICAGO MEAT PACKERS &
HENRY J BEANS
My Kinda Town Ltd
5 Raphael Street
London SW7 1DL
Tel: 071 581 7933
11 Restaurants including
Aberdeen, Belfast,
Dublin, Glasgow,
London, Manchester.

DAMON'S -
THE PLACE FOR RIBS
999 Doddington Road
Lincoln LN6 1XX
Tel: 0522 500878

THE DEADWOOD STAGE
Bank House Hotel
11 Bank Street
Wakefield
Yorkshire WE1 1EH
Tel: 0924 368248

DEAN'S DINER
28 Collingwood Street
Newcastle Upon Tyne
NE1 1JF
Tel: 091 232 0358

DI MAGGIO'S BAR & DELI
BASEMENT
21 Royal Exchange Square
Glasgow G2
Tel: 041 248 2111

GREAT AMERICAN INVENTIONS

1965 – Earlybird, the world's first communications satellite, was launched.
1969 – In July Americans Neil Armstrong (the very first) and Edwin 'Buzz' Aldrin became the first men to walk on the moon. They arrived courtesy of Apollo 11 and the Lunar Module.

DINER 77
77 Pontcanna Street
Cardiff
Tel: 0222 344628

DOMINO'S PIZZA
85 outlets nationwide
Call Directory Inquiries 192
or Head Office Tel: 0908 618222

ED'S DINER
12 Moor Street
London W1
Tel: 071-352-1956

362 Kings Road
London SW3
Tel: 071 352 1956

FATBOY'S DINER
21/22 Maiden Lane
Covent Garden
London WC2E
Tel: 071 240 1902

296 Bishopsgate
London EC2 4QX
Tel: 071 375 2763

FAT SAM'S
Forte Crest Hotel
Cardiff CF1 2XB
Tel: 0222 388681

FAT SAM'S AMAZIN'
PIZZA PIE FACTORY
56 Fountainbridge Road
Edinburgh EH3 9PY
Tel: 031 228 3111

GREAT AMERICAN INVENTIONS

1913 – Formica, the rigid, decorated laminated plastic, was invented. (The same year also saw the introduction of Camel cigarettes.) In its early days laminate, available in an uninspiring palette of browns, was used as an insulating material for electrical and industrial products such as radio parts and the much-prized new electric starters on cars. However, its potential as a durable, wipe-clean surface material coupled with falling production costs and its availability in a rainbow of bright colours, soon led to its use on acres of tables and counters in a million diners, cafés and kitchens. Upmarket applications included its extensive use in the interiors of the ocean liner HMS Queen Mary. Famous designers commissioned to produce fashionable patterns included Raymond Loewy – the boomerang-inspired squiggles of his 'Skylark' remained a favourite for years.

FILLING STATION
235 High Street
Edinburgh EH1 1PE
Tel: 031 226 2488

FUDDRUCKLES
4A Moss Lane
Altrincham
Cheshire WA14 1BA
Tel: 061 941 2065

HARD ROCK CAFE
150 Old Park Lane
London W1Y 3LJ
Tel: 071 629 0382

HENRY J BEAN'S BAR & GRILL
Head Office
5 Raphael Street
London SW7 1DL
Tel: 071 581 7933

THE HUNGRY COWBOY
20 Bedford Street
London WC2E 9HP
Tel: 071 240 2971

JEFFERSON'S
563 Hagley Road West
Quinton
Birmingham B23 1LJ
Tel: 021 422 2515

JOE SMO'S
29 Chiswick High Road
London W4
Tel: 081 995 0945

JOHNNY ROCKET'S
140 Fulham Road
London SW10 9PY
Tel: 071 370 2794

KENNY'S
70 Heath Street
London NW3 1DN
Tel: 071 435 6972
Cajun & Creole Cuisine

KENTUCKY FRIED
CHICKEN
Over 300 restaurants nationwide.
See Local Directory for nearest
branch.

LA PERGOLA
66 Streatham High Road
London SW16
Tel: 081 769 2646
Elvis Look-a-like Cabaret Nightly.

LONG ISLAND ICED TEA SHOP
1 Upper Street
St Martin's Lane
London WC2 9EA
Tel: 071 240 3734

MAE'S DINER
Blue Boar Motorways Ltd
Rotherthorpe Services
Southbound M1
Northants NN4 9QY
Tel: 0327 78811

MADOGS
38A George Street
Edinburgh
Tel: 031 225 3408

MAMMA'S AMERICAN PIZZA &
PANZEROFFI
28/30 The Grassmarket
Edinburgh EH1 2JU
Tel: 031 225 6464

McDONALD'S
500 restaurants nationwide
McDonald's Restaurants Ltd
11-59 High Road
East Finchley
London N2 8AW
Tel: 081 883 6400

MILNER'S DINER
12 Russell Hill Road
Purley
Surrey CR2 2LA
Tel: 081 763 2526

MINSKY'S DINER
70 The Mall
Ealing
London W5 5LS
Tel: 081 567 5237

NEW YORK DELI
18 High Street Arcade
Cardiff CF1 1BB
Tel: 0222 388388

OLD ORLEANS
The Chef & Brewer Group
PO Box 112
Riverside House
Riverside Way
Northampton NN1 5NU
Tel: 0604-612161
Brings a taste of the American 'deep
south' to the UK at 17 restaurants
nationwide including London,
Edinburgh, Cardiff.

PAPPA'S GREAT AMERICAN EATS
7 Victoria Street
Edinburgh EH1 2HE
Tel: 031 225 7306

PLANET HOLLYWOOD
Coventry Street
London W1V 7DD
Tel: 071 287 1000

SMOLLENSKY'S BALLOON
1 Dover Street
London W1X 3PJ
Tel: 071 491 1199

SMOLLENSKY'S ON THE
STRAND
105 The Strand
London WC2R OAA
Tel: 071 497 2101

STARVIN MARVIN'S
Trafford Road
Salford Quays
Salford
Tel: 061 877 8077

GREAT AMERICAN INVENTIONS

1853 - The first potato chip was
created. Chef George Crum of
Moon's Lake Lodge, Saratoga,
New York, is credited with
the invention of the world's
favourite snack. Americans had
already discovered the delights
of the chunky fried tuber, but
Chef Crum decided to go for
finesse and sliced the spud
thinly to create what he called
Saratoga chips.

STUDEBAKER'S
Broad Street
Birmingham B1

TACO BELL
194 Earl's Court Road
London SW5 9QF
Tel: 071 373 1011

TGI FRIDAY
12 restaurants including Cardiff, Coventry, Fareham, Glasgow.
Head Office
Bouverie House
200 Silbury Boulevard
Milton Keynes MK1 1LG
Tel: 0908 669911

WENDY'S
25-27 Shaftsbury Avenue
London W1V 7HA
Tel: 071 434 1390

341-349 Oxford Street
London W1R 1HB
Tel: 071 499 2199

WESTCOAST DINER
Welsh Back
Bristol BS1 4SB
Tel: 0272 291959

CARS

AMERICAN CAR
IMPORTS LTD
57 Coburg Road
Wood Green
London N22 6UB
Tel: 081 889 4545

AMERICAN 50'S CAR HIRE
Claygate
Enfield Road
Shotgate
Wickford
Essex SS11 8SZ
Tel: 0268 735914

AMERICAN CARWASH
COMPANY
78 Pancras Road
London NW1 1UJ
Tel: 071 387 2832

AMERICAN LIMOUSINE HIRE
11 Exeter Close
Folkestone
Kent CT19 4JD
Tel: 0303 277769

THE AMERICAN LIMOUSINE
COMPANY
Newdigate Place
Newdigate
Surrey RH5 5BP
Tel: 0293 871335

BAUER MILLETT & CO. LTD
5 Peter Street
Manchester M2 5QR
Tel: 061-831-7447
UK's only Cadillac Dealership

CAROLINA CLASSICS
Whitchurch
Shropshire SY13 2JJ
Tel: 0948 74508

CLASSIC AMERICAN
CAR HIRE
Mount Pleasant
Hornsea
N. Humberside
HU18 1DX
Tel: 0964 535341

CLASSIC CARS
Avenue House
Jesmond
Newcastle Upon Tyne
NE2 2QU
Tel: 091 281 4001

DREAM CARS
8-10 Ingate Place
London SW8 3NS
Tel: 071 627 5775

FRANKIES YANKEE'S
1770 Pershore Road
Cotteridge
Birmingham B30 3BG
Tel: 021 458 7000

FUTURAMIC
AMERICAN CARS
4 Paget Close
Needham Market
Ipswich IP6 8XF
Tel: 0449 722324

STRAIGHT EIGHT LTD
152/160 Goldhawk Road
London W12 8HJ
Tel: 081 743 1599

TUCKER'S USA CARS
142 Meldreth Road
Whaddon
Royston
Herts SG8 5RP
Tel: 0223 207324

MOTORCYCLES

ALVIN'S MOTORCYCLES
9A/9B Springfield Street
Edinburgh EH6 5EF
Tel: 031 555 1039

DUBLIN HARLEY-DAVIDSON
24/25 Blessington Street
Dublin 7
Tel: (010) 3531 303000

THE FOUNDARY
Broad Oak Road
Canterbury
Kent CT2 7QG
Tel: 0227 463986

HARLEY-DAVIDSON-45
SUPPLIES
Mill Loft
Mill Street
Broadway
Weymouth
Dorset DT3 5DP
Tel: 0305 813480
Obsolete parts for H-D 1937-52

HARLEY-DAVIDSON OF
SOUTHPORT
153 East Bank Street
Southport
Merseyside PR8 1EE
Tel: 0704 543745

THE HARLEY SHOP
Harley House
Whitwood
Castleford
West Yorkshire WF10 5PD
Tel: 0977 517566

INDIAN OWNERS CLUB
Contact: John Chatterton
183 Buxton Road
Newtown
New Mills
Stockport
Cheshire SK12 3LA
Tel: 0663 747106

INDIAN RIDERS ASSOCIATION
Contact: Mrs S DeBidaph
Mallydams Court
Hall Drive
Martineau Lane
Fairlight
East Sussex TN35 5DR
Tel: 0424 812820

MOTEX LTD
Shire Business Park
Warndon
Worcester
Hereford & Worcester WR4 9FD
Tel: 0905 756883

MOTOLUX
5 Scotland Street Lane West
Edinburgh EH3 6PT
Tel: 031 557 5807
Britain's only Indian Bikes dealer.

RIDERS (BRIDGWATER) LTD
Riders House
Wylds Road
Bridgwater
Somerset TA6 4BH
Tel: 0278 457652

SAINT PETER PORT GARAGES
Trinity Square
St Peter Port
Guernsey
Tel: 0481 724261

SEQUANA CYCLES
1 Farthingloe Cottages
Folkestone Road
Dover CT15 7AA
Tel: 0304 242656

SURREY HARLEY-DAVIDSON
Unit 5, Havenbury Estate
Sation Road
Dorking
Surrey RH4 1ES
Tel: 0306 883825

THREE CROSS MOTORCYCLES
Woolsbridge Industrial Estate
Three Legged Cross
Wimborne
Dorset BH21 6SP
Tel: 0202 824531

FH WARR & SONS
104 Waterford Road
London SW6 2EU
Tel: 071 736 2934

WHEELS INTERNATIONAL
Watling Street
Hockliffe
Bedfordshire LU7 9LS
Tel: 0525 210130

WINDY CORNER
8 Moat Way
Barwell
Leicestershire
LE9 8EY
Tel: 0455 842922

ULTIMATE PERFORMANCE
Unit 6/7 Sandringham Mews
Ealing
London W5 5DG
Tel: 081 579 5065

GREAT AMERICAN INVENTIONS

1909 – The Model T Ford appeared. This succeeded the Model N and was the first motor car to be mass-produced. The assembly of parts – groundbreaking in its use of a continuous line moving at a steady rate past groups of workers who put together the collection of standardised parts – borrowed directly from mechanised American slaughterhouses. A staggering fifteen million Model T cars were driven off the production line in the ensuing twenty years.

SPORTS & LEISURE

AMERICAN FOOTBALL
NFL World League
Cumberland House
26/100 Scrubs Lane
London NW10 6AH
Tel: 081 964 2244

BRITISH CHEERLEADING
ASSOCIATION
102 White Horse Road
Windsor
Berks SL4 4PH
Tel: 0753 86713

BASEBALL
BRITISH BASEBALL FEDERATION
66 Belverdere Road
Hessle
North Humberside
HU13 9JJ
Tel: 0482 643551
Send SAE for Factsheet.

BASKETBALL
BASKETBALL ASSOCIATION
OF WALES
Connies House
Rhymeney River Bridge Road
Cardiff CF3 7YZ
Tel: 0222 454395

ENGLISH BASKETBALL
ASSOCIATION
48 Bradford Road
Stanningley
Leeds LS28 6DF
Tel: 0532 361166

IRISH BASKETBALL
ASSOCIATION
c/o National Basketball Arena
Tymon Park
Dublin 24
Tel: 010 35315 90211

SCOTTISH BASKETBALL
ASSOCIATION
Caledonia House
South Gyle
Edinburgh EH12 9DQ
Tel: 031 317 7260

DRAG RACING
SANTA POD RACE CLUB
National Drag Ways
Unit 6E
1st Floor
101 Farm Lane
London SW6 1QJ
Tel: 071 386 8777

ICE HOCKEY
BRITISH ICE HOCKEY
ASSOCIATION
Tel: 0202 303946

SKATE ATTACK LTD.
95 Highgate Road
London NW5 1TR
Tel: 071 267 6961
For all information on Street and Ice
Hockey

SKATE ATTACK HOCKEY
MUSEUM
Alexandra Palace Ice Rink
Alexandra Palace Park
Wood Green
London N22

SURFING
BRITISH SURFING
ASSOCIATION
Champion's Yard
Penzance
Cornwall TR18 2TA
Tel: 0736 60250

LOW PRESSURE
186 Kensington Park Road
London W11 1EF
Tel: 071 792 3134

TEN PIN BOWLING
HOLLYWOOD BOWL LTD
Elliot Street
Finnieston
Glasgow C3 8HY
Tel: 041 248 4478
Centres in Blackburn, Bolton, Carlisle,
Glasgow, Hartlepool, Keighley,
Liverpool, Loughborough, Margate,
Sterling, Tottenham, Torquay.

LA BOWL
Quattro Leisure Ltd
Sweet Street
Leeds LS11 9DB
Tel: 0532 442013
Centres in Isle of Wight, Leeds,
Warrington.

TEN PIN BOWLING
PROPRIETORS
ASSOCIATION
72 Queens Road
Loughton
Essex IG10 1RS
Tel: 081 508 7000

VOLLEY BALL
ENGLISH VOLLEYBALL
ASSOCIATION
27 South Road
West Bridgford
Nottingham NG2 7AG
Tel: 0602 816324

RECREATIONAL VEHICLES

AMERICAN MOTORHOME
CLUB
2 The Triangle
Peasehill Road
Ripley
Derbyshire DE5 3JG
Tel: 0773 744817

DUDLEY'S AMERICAN
MOTOR HOMES LTD
37 West End
Witney
Oxon OX8 6NH
Tel: 0993 703774

THEME PARKS

ALTON TOWERS
Alton
Staffordshire
ST10 4DB
Tel: 0538 702200

AMERICAN ADVENTURE
Pit Lane
Ilkeston
Derbyshire DE7 5SX
Tel: 0773 531521

CAMELOT
Charnock Richard
Chorley
NR Preston
Lancashire PR7 5LP
Tel: 0257 453044

FRONTIERLAND
Marine Road Central
Morecombe LA4 4DG
Tel: 0524 410024

GRANADA STUDIOS TOUR
Water Street
Manchester M60 9EA
Tel: 061 833 0880

THORPE PARK
Staines Road
Chertsey
Surrey KT16 8PN
Tel: 0932 569393

CINEPLEXES
UCI UNITED CINEMAS
Located at: Bayswater, Bracknell,
Clydebank, Coollock, Derby,
Dudley, East Kilbride, Edinburgh,
Gateshead, Hatfield, Hull, Milton
Keynes, Poole, Portsmouth,
Sheffield, Solihull, Sutton,
Swansea, Tallaght, Tamworth,
Telford, Warrington, Wycombe,
West Thurrock, Wycombe,
See Local Press for details.

WARNER BROS.
MULTIPLEX CINEMAS
Located at: Basingstoke,
Bury, Doncaster,
Newcastle-Upon-Tyne,
Preston, Meadowhall
Sheffield, Thurrock Lakeside
Essex, York.
See Local Press for details.

SHOPPING MALLS

ARNDALE CENTRE
Arndale House
Manchester M4 3AA
Tel: 061 833 9851

CRYSTAL PEAKS SHOPPING
CENTRE
Eckington Way, Sothall
Sheffield S19 6PQ
Tel: 0743 510457

BRENT CROSS SHOPPING
CENTRE
London NW4 3FP
Tel: 081 202 8095

LAKESIDE SHOPPING CENTRE
West Thurrock, Grays
Essex RM16 1WT
Tel: 0708 869933

MEADOWHALL SHOPPING
CENTRE
1 The Oasis
Sheffield SH9 1ED
Tel: 0742 569999

METRO CENTRE
Gateshead
Tyne & Wear NE11 9YG
Tel: 091 493 2040

OLYMPIA SHOPPING CENTRE
Rothesay Street
East Kilbride G74 1PG

PAVILLION SHOPPING CENTRE
New Street
Birmingham B4 7FL
Tel: 021 631 4121

GREAT AMERICAN INVENTIONS

1942 – Earl Tupper began
producing thin-walled, clip-top
polythene containers called
Tupperware. The company started
home-selling parties because
customers didn't know how to use
the product when they saw it
stacked on the shelves in shops. As
much an innovation as the
colourful plastic containers
themselves, Tupperware parties
began with games and giggles and
ended with very successful bouts
of buying. Tupperware, perfect for
storing leftovers, became standard
in the rapidly multiplying
refrigerators of the 1950s.

MUSIC & DANCE

BARN DANCE AGENCY
62 Beechwood Road
South Croydon
Surrey CR2 OAA
Tel: 081 657 2813

BIDDS COUNTRY
MUSIC CLUB
Sutherland Road
Longton
Stoke on Trent ST3 1JB
Tel: 0782 310527
Purpose built Country Music Venue

BRITISH COUNTRY
MUSIC ASSOCIATION
Information Service For Country
Music Fans
PO Box 240
Harrow
Middlesex HA3 7PH
Tel: 0273 559 750

CROSBY HEAD PUB
243 Old Street
London EC1V 9EY
Tel: 071 253 1239

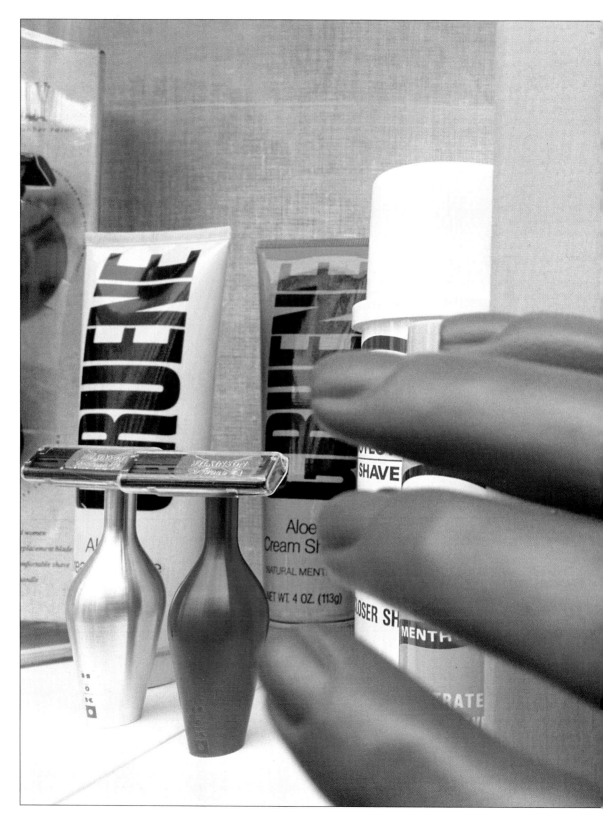

GRAND OLE OPRY
2/4 Govan Road
Glasgow G51 1HS
Tel: 041 429 5396

LONESOME NO MORE
Rails
Euston Concourse
Eversholt Street
London NW1
2nd Thursday each month.

MADDY'S JIVING SCHOOL
PO Box 2149
London W13 9XF
Tel: 081 566 5226

ROCK 'N' ROLL RECORD HOP
Notre Dame Hall
Leicester Square
London WC2
Tel: 081 663 6355
Alternate Saturdays

THE 3R'S CLUB
Reading Rock 'N' Roll Club
103 Bourne Road
Pangbourne
Reading
Tel: 0734 842664

UK COUNTRY-LINE
The Definitive British Country Music
news and information service.
Tel: 0891 800633

WEAVERS
98 Newington Green Road
London N1 4RG
Tel: 071 226 6911

GREAT AMERICAN INVENTIONS

1924 – Rayon was first
manufactured from cellulose to
imitate silk. It was followed
before the end of the decade by
the Du Pont Company's
development of nylon. Both
materials revolutionised the
clothing industry, allowing the
mass production of inexpensive,
lightweight, easy-care garments.

MAGAZINES & NEWSPAPERS

THE AMERICAN
Published fortnightly:
114-115 West Street
Farnham
Surrey GU9 7HL
Tel: 0252 713366

AMERICAN IN LONDON
Published bi-monthly by:
Niki Michaelides
93-97 Bushey Mill Lane
Watford
Herts WD2 4JG
Tel: 0923 210046

ANGLO-AMERICAN SPORTS
Priory House
85 Priory Grove
London SW8 2PD
Tel: 071 720 6456

CJ JEEP CLUB (UK)
For Real Jeep Owners, by Jeep Owners
Mark Askew
42 Howden Close
Bessacarr
Doncaster
South Yorkshire DN4 7JW
Tel: 0302 538200

ALL AMERICAN HEROES
BACK STREET HEROES
CLASSIC AMERICAN
Published by: Myatt McFarlane plc
PO Box 666
Altrincham
Cheshire WA14 2UD
Tel: 061 928 3480
Magazines for car & motorcycle
enthusiasts.

JUKEBOX JOURNAL
PO Box 545
Brighton BN1 4HU
Fax: 0273 677922

LONESOME NO MORE
112c Agar Grove
Camden Town
London NW1 9TY
Country Music Magazine

PINBALL PLAYER
Pinball Owners Association
PO Box 2
Haslemere
Surrey GU27 2EQ
Magazine for pinball enthusiasts.

COMIC BOOKSTORES

DEAD HEAD COMICS
44 Victoria Street
Edinburgh EH1 2JW
Tel: 031 226 2774

DYNAMIC COMICS
Units 43-47
In Shops Centre
68 Church Street
Croydon
Surrey CR0 1RB
Tel: 081 681 2597

FORBIDDEN PLANET
71 New Oxford Street
London WC1A 1DG
Tel: 071 379 6042

5 Duke Street
Cardiff CF1 2AY
Tel: 0222 228885

HAPPY PLANET
85 Westgate
Bradford
West Yorkshire
BD1 2RD
Tel: 0274 736292

NOSTALGIA & COMICS
14-16 Smallbrook
Queensway
Birmingham
B5 4EN
Tel: 021 643 0143

ODYSSEY 7
Precinct Centre
Oxford Road
Manchester
M13 9RN
Tel: 061 273 6666

TOP 10 SOHO
Unit 3
9-12 St Anne's Court
London W1V 3AX
Tel: 071 734 7388

THE VINTAGE
MAGAZINE CO LTD.
39/43 Brewer Street
London W1R 3FD
Tel: 071 439 8525

247 Camden High Street
London NW1
Tel: 071 482 0587

THE DISNEY STORE

Union Street
Bath BA1 1RW
Tel: 0225 429853

The Pavillion Shopping Centre
Birmingham B4 7SL
Tel: 021 631 4121

Broadmead Street
Bristol BS1 3EA
Tel: 0272 297777

The Glades Shopping Centre
Bromley BR1 1DD
Tel: 081 466 1640

County Mall
Crawley RH10 1FF
Tel: 0293 528282

Whitgift Centre
Croydon CR0 1US
Tel: 081 649 9349

Bentalls Centre
Kingston
Tel: 081 549 5469

Clayton Square Shopping Centre
Liverpool L1 1QR
Tel: 051 708 7010

Regent Street
London W1R 5SA
Tel: 071 287 6558

Brent Cross Shopping Centre
London NW4 3FP
Tel: 081 202 0082

St Ann's Square
Manchester M2 2HA
Tel: 061 832 4361

> GREAT AMERICAN INVENTIONS
>
> 1939 – Nylon stockings appeared on the market, to replace their expensive silk forebears, just in time for thousands of GIs to woo their newfound British girlfriends.

The Old Corner Pin
Nottingham NG1 3ED
Tel: 0602 484808

Meadowhall Centre
Sheffield S9 1EP
Tel: 0742 569333

The Harlequin Centre
Watford WD1 2TL
Tel: 0923 223399

Lakeside Shopping Centre
West Thurrock RM16 1ZF
Tel: 0708 890916

Princes Street
Edinburgh EH2 2AN
Tel: 031 557 2772

St Enoch Centre
Glasgow G73 3LX
Tel: 041 248 1441

JUKE BOXES & SLOT MACHINES

BEYST JUKEBOX COMPANY
Muckton Bottom
Louth
Lincolnshire LN11 8NT
Tel: 0507 480385

COLLECTABLE JUKEBOXES,
SLOTS & NEONS
PO Box 1964
Selly Oak
Birmingham
B29 4BZ
Tel: 021 475 6540

JUKEBOX DELUXE
Stone Cottage
Beenham
Reading RG7 5NN
TEl: 0734 713341

JUKEBOX SHOP
14 High Street
Lye
Stourbridge
West Midlands DY9 8JT
Tel: 0384 424325

THE LIGHTNING CENTRE
676 High Road
Finchley
London N12 9PT
Tel: 071 445 1765
Original USA 1950s' Telephones &
Coke Machines.

MUSIC MAKERS
13 East Square
Basildon
Essex SS14 1HT

Unit 420
Third Floor
Lakeside Shopping Centre
West Thurrock
Essex RM16 1WT
Tel: 0708 869933

PINBALL PARADISE
Unit 1
Greysmere Mews
Beacon Hill Road
Beacon Hill
Surrey GU26 6NR
Tel: 0428 606116

SOUND LEISURE
6 Stafford Street
Leeds LS10 1NN
Tel: 0532 772484

AMERICAN SCHOOLS

AMERICAN COMMUNITY
SCHOOL
Hillingdon Court
Vine Lane
Hillingdon
Middlesex UB10 0BE
Tel: 0895 259771

AMERICAN COMMUNITY
SCHOOL
Heywood
Portsmouth Road
Cobham
Surrey KT11 1BL
Tel: 0932 867251

AMERICAN SCHOOL IN
ABERDEEN
Craigton Road
Cults
Aberdeen AB1 9QD
Tel: 0224 868927

AMERICAN SCHOOL IN
LONDON
2-8 Loudoun Road
London NW8 0NP
Tel: 071 722 0101

TASIS ENGLAND AMERICAN
SCHOOL
Coldharbour Lane
Thorpe
Surrey TW20 8TE
Tel: 0932 565252

GREAT AMERICAN INVENTIONS

1957 – Jack Kilby devised the first
silicon chip. This integrated
electrical circuit on a slice of
silicon crystal has been a major
contributor to the proliferation of
such technological innovations as
the calculator and computer.
1977 – The Apple personal
computer appeared from the small
garage-based company founded by
electronics engineers Steven Jobs
and Stephen Wozniak.

FOOD

BASKIN ROBBINS ICE CREAM
Head Office
Sutherland House
3 Dukes Meadow
Millboard Road
Bourne End
Buckinghamshire SL8 5FX
Tel: 0682 531531
75 Outlets Nationwide

BAGEL EXPRESS
62 Fleet Street
London EC4Y 1JU
Tel: 071 353 0761

DUNKIN DONUTS
Head Office
48 Carnaby Street
London W1V 1PF
Tel: 071 287 5195
4 stores and outlets at 7/11,
Mobil & Texaco.

RECORD STORES

BEANO'S
27 Surrey Street
Croydon CRO 1RR
Tel: 081 649 8181
Original, rare and jukebox records.

BUD'S COUNTRY MUSIC STORE
184 High Street
Penge
London SE20 7QB
Tel: 081 676 8801

RECORD CORNER
27 Bedford Hill
Balham
London SW12 9EX
Tel: 081 673 9192

TOWER RECORDS
1 Piccadilly Circus
London W1V 9LA
Tel: 071 439 2500

GREAT AMERICAN INVENTIONS

1903 – Wilbur and Orville
Wright made the first successful
powered flight in a heavier-than-
air machine at Kill Devil Hill near
Kitty Hawk, North Carolina.
After a number of spectacular
failures by aviation pioneers, the
brothers succeeded in getting their
flimsy-looking craft, the 600 lb
gasoline-powered Flyer, off the
ground. Thirty-two-year-old
Orville was at the helm for all 12
seconds of the first flight.

HÄAGEN DAZ ICE CREAM
Head Office
Runnymede House
Heriot Road
Chertsey
Surrey KT16 9DT
Tel: 0932 570011
18 outlets including Edinburgh,
London, Windsor.

EVENTS

THE CHELSEA CRUISE
Classic American Car Cruise, the last
Saturday in every month.
Battersea Park
London SW11

JUKEBOX MADNESS
Annual show for Jukebox and Pinball
Machine dealers and collectors.
Held in Hounslow each October.
For further details contact:
Mike Trussell
Tel: 0734 713341

HEMSBY ROCK 'N' ROLL
WEEKENDER
Annual Rock 'n' Roll Weekender. For
further details contact:
PO Box 36
Beckenham
Kent BR3 3SN
Tel: 081 663 6355

MEMORABILIA

ALF'S AMERICANA
Tel: 081 505 7347
Advertising signs, license plates, hubcaps.

BYGONE TIMES
Grove Mill
The Green
Eccleston
Lancashire PR7 5PD
Tel: 0257 453780
Americana, architectural pieces, neon signs, cars and motorbikes.

CHAPMAN'S AMERICANA
The Old School House
Nash
Milton Keynes MK17 0ES
Tel: 0908 502272
Gas pump globes, enamel and tin signs, Coca Cola memorabillia, 50s fridges.

DECODENCE
13 The Mall
Camden Passage
London N1 0PD
Tel: 071 354 4473
Classic 1930s & 40s American bakelite products.

THE PERIOD PETROL PUMP CO.
Grove Farm, Mill Green
Burston, Diss
Norfolk IP22 3TH
Tel: 0379 643978

RUSH MARKETING
17 Gilpin Way
Olney
Bucks MK46 4DN
Tel: 0234 240712
Reproduction enamel advertising signs.

GREAT AMERICAN INVENTIONS

1929 – Raymond Loewy designed the casing for the Gestetner duplicating machine, choosing bakelite as the sheath material. It was a significant design development that hid the working parts of the machine, acknowledging that operators were uninterested in, and needed no knowledge of, the mechanics. Loewy described the job (for which he used clay, he claimed, for the first time in a prototype) as 'a facelift'; it survived, with minor streamlining modifications, until the 1950s.

1933 – Walter Dorwin Teague designed the classic streamlined Baby Brownie camera for Kodak. Portraiture and the recording of family events became available to the masses for the first time.

BIBLIOGRAPHY

Bedixson, T. and Platt, J.: Milton Keynes: Image and Reality, Granta Editions.
Eco, Umberto: Travels in Hyperreality, Picador.
Emery, Michael C. and Smythe, Ted C.: Mass Communication, Wm C. Brown.
Gardner, Carl and Sheppard, Julie: Consuming Passions, Unwin Hyman.
Hughes, Robert: Culture of Complaint, OUP.
Jellicoe, Geoffrey and Susan: The Landscape of Man, Thames and Hudson.
Jencks, Charles: Architecture Today, Academy Editions.
Jencks, Charles: Post-Modern Triumphs in London, Academy Editions.
King, Anthony D.: Global Cities, Routledge.
Kostof, Spiro: The City Shaped, Thames and Hudson.
Lewis, Peter: The Fifties: Portrait of an Age, Cupid.
Maclancy, Jeremy: Consuming Culture, Chapmans.
Marc, David: Prime Time, Prime Movers, Boston.
Marcus, Greil: Dead Elvis, Penguin.
Mingo, Jack: The Official Couch Potato Handbook, San Francisco.
Moss, Norman: British/American Dictionary, Hutchinson.
Naremore, James and Brantlinger, Patrick eds: Modernity and Mass Culture, Indiana University Press.
O'Rourke, P.J.: Holidays in Hell, Picador.
Park, James ed: Cultural Icons, Bloomsbury.
Pulos, Arthur J.: The American Design Adventure, MIT Press.
Ritzer, George: The McDonaldization of Society, Pine Forge.
Salmieri, Stephen and Edwards, Owen: Cadillac, Tabard Press.
Shields, Rob ed: Lifestyle Shopping, Routledge.
Walmsley, Jane: Brit-Think, Ameri-Think, Harrap.

ACKNOWLEDGEMENTS

Thanks to Simon Weitzman of Vamp Films,
Jon Gibson of SOM, Fay Sweet,
Tony Catanzaro and David Barrie.